The persistence of poverty across generations

Available in alternative formats

This publication can be provided in alternative formats, such as large print, Braille, audiotape and on disk. Please contact: Communications Department, Joseph Rowntree Foundation, The Homestead, 40 Water End, York YO30 6WP. Tel: 01904 615905. Email: info@jrf.org.uk

The persistence of poverty across generations

A view from two British cohorts

Jo Blanden and Steve Gibbons

JOSEPH ROWNTREE
FOUNDATION

First published in Great Britain in April 2006 by

The Policy Press
Fourth Floor, Beacon House
Queen's Road
Bristol BS8 1QU
UK

Tel no +44 (0)117 331 4054
Fax no +44 (0)117 331 4093
E-mail tpp-info@bristol.ac.uk
www.policypress.org.uk

Published for the Joseph Rowntree Foundation by The Policy Press

ISBN-10 1 86134 852 5
ISBN-13 978 1 86134 852 4

British Library Cataloguing in Publication Data
A catalogue record for this book is available from the British Library.

Library of Congress Cataloging-in-Publication Data
A catalog record for this book has been requested.

Jo Blanden is a lecturer in economics at the University of Surrey, UK, and **Steve Gibbons** is a lecturer in economic geography in the Department of Geography and Environment at the London School of Economics and Political Science (LSE), UK. Both authors are research associates in LSE's Centre for Economic Performance.

The **Joseph Rowntree Foundation** has supported this project as part of its programme of research and innovative development projects, which it hopes will be of value to policy makers, practitioners and service users. The facts presented and views expressed in this report are, however, those of the authors and not necessarily those of the Foundation.

Cover design by Qube Design Associates, Bristol
Printed in Great Britain by Hobbs the Printers Ltd, Southampton

Contents

List of figures and tables

Figures

Tables

Acknowledgements

This project was supported by the Joseph Rowntree Foundation, and we particularly thank Chris Goulden of the JRF for all his help in supervising the project. We would also like to thank our Project Advisory Group for their help and advice throughout.

Members of the Project Advisory Group:

Jennie Van Den Berg (Department for Work and Pensions)
Stephen Jenkins (Institute for Social and Economic Research, University of Essex)
Heather Joshi (Centre for Longitudinal Studies, University of London)
Paul Dornan (Child Poverty Action Group)
Kirby Swales (Office of the Deputy Prime Minister)
Alissa Goodman (Institute for Fiscal Studies)

Summary

This report examines the magnitude of the link between child poverty and poverty later in adult life using members of two British cohorts, one group in their teens in the 1970s and the other in their teens in the 1980s.

The core data we use is on income and other characteristics at age 16 for both cohorts, as well as information on later income and characteristics at age 33 for the first cohort and age 30 for the second cohort. We are also able to use information on income at age 42 for the older group.

The questions we address are:

- How large is the transmission of poverty between a teenager's parents' circumstances and their own circumstances when they are in their early 30s?
- By how much has the strength of this transmission of poverty changed between the two cohorts who were teenagers in the 1970s and the 1980s?
- How far do other characteristics at age 16 and in adulthood explain these links?
- How far do the effects of early disadvantage continue to be felt as individuals reach middle age? (This can be considered by looking at outcomes at age 42 for those who were teenagers in the 1970s.)

Our results find evidence of a significant persistence of poverty from teenhood to the early thirties. This persistence is measured by the odds ratio. This is obtained by comparing the chances (or odds) of being poor if one's parents are poor with the chances of being poor if they are not.

Our results show that teenage poverty doubled the odds of being poor adults for teenagers growing up in the 1970s. It is also possible to use the data to discover the relationship between teenage poverty and poverty at age 42 for this group. We find that being poor as a teenager in the 1970s doubled the odds of being poor in early middle age at the beginning of the millennium. Teenage poverty is as strongly related to middle age poverty as it was to poverty in earlier adulthood.

This is perhaps surprising because we might expect the influence of teenage poverty to fade as the years go by. One explanation could be that teenage poverty influences poverty in early adulthood, and this then links through to poverty in later life. There may not necessarily be a direct link from teenage poverty to middle age once we take account of this. Our results show that the connection between poverty as a teenager and in middle age is strong and cannot be explained by links with poverty status at age 33. It is therefore clear that the link between poverty in teenhood and adulthood continues through to middle age, regardless of whether or not a person is recorded as poor in their thirties. It is also clear that the association between poverty at different points in adulthood is much stronger than between childhood poverty and adult poverty.

Understanding why poverty persists

It is extremely difficult to pin down the factors that *cause* the persistence of poverty. Income poverty goes hand-in-hand with numerous other forms of deprivation, some of which are consequences of the lack of resources in the household and others that lead to poverty in themselves. Many of these aspects of deprivation may be a result of other underlying factors that are very hard to measure and persist throughout individuals' lives. For all these reasons, it is extremely difficult to fully understand the causal processes that lie at the route of the persistence of poverty through the lifecycle.

We gain some understanding of how poverty is transmitted across generations by examining the link between teenage poverty and adult poverty when the other characteristics of the child's family are held constant. This enables us to find out whether it is disadvantage in general, rather than income poverty, that is harming children's life-chances. It also enables the analysis of which aspects of disadvantage are particularly harmful.

The results of this exercise make it clear that *poor teenagers in the 1970s grew up to be poor because of more general family background disadvantages*, in particular parental non-employment and low education – poverty itself had little or no direct effect over and above these teenage family factors. However, *for teenagers in the 1980s, poverty had a direct effect on the chances of ending up in poverty, even allowing for differences in these same aspects of family background*. Certainly, family background differences account for much of the persistence from child poverty to adulthood, but the odds of a poor teenager being a poor adult were still much larger than for a non-poor teenager. This provides some grounds for suggesting that redistribution could have had a beneficial impact for those growing up in the later cohort.

A similar analysis tells us which adult characteristics help to explain the persistence of poverty between teenhood and adulthood. Unsurprisingly, being out of work, having a partner out of work or having little accumulated work history are the factors most closely associated with poverty – both for adults in middle age and in their thirties – although low education plays an important role too. Our understanding of the persistence of poverty can be improved by analysing which of these characteristics are most closely linked with disadvantage and poverty in the teenage years.

We find that earlier disadvantage is associated with all of these later outcomes. One of the reasons for the stronger persistence in the second period is that teenage poverty became more closely linked to the likelihood of a person being out of work in their early thirties. The main factors linked to being out of work in adulthood are low education, lone parenthood and ill health. However, educational attainment does not explain the rise in persistence: the risk of poor teenagers in the 1980s ending up without qualifications was not much greater than for poor teenagers in the 1970s. Compared with a girl in the 1970s, a poor teenage girl in the 1980s was at higher risk for lone parenthood, and at higher risk for incapacity through illness in her thirties. These facts can explain part, although not all, of the rise in the intergenerational persistence over this period – but only for women.

This report presents two main new findings on the extent of the persistence of poverty. The first is that the persistence of poverty from the teens into the early thirties has risen over time, with teenage poverty having a greater impact on later outcomes for teenagers in the 1980s compared with teenagers in the 1970s. This finding adds to the wider evidence that family background has had a growing impact on later outcomes between these cohorts.

The second major finding shows that the link between poverty in teenhood and adulthood continues to have a bearing through to middle age for the cohort who were teenagers in the 1970s (born in 1958). This is the case regardless of whether or not the person was poor in their thirties. In other words, an adult who was a poor teenager continues to be at higher risk of poverty by middle age even if they were out of poverty in their thirties.

The findings on *why* poverty persists are less clear-cut, and reveal multidimensional causes. The results suggest that initiatives to improve skills and employment opportunities are probably the only sensible way to tackle the problem of persistent poverty and that there is no quick fix available through other more specific interventions. Despite the lack of specific policy prescriptions that can be drawn, it is clear that children in poverty are more likely to grow up to be poor. Our results therefore highlight the importance of the policy agenda to reduce child poverty and disadvantage, although our work on unpicking the causes of poverty persistence indicates that income transfers alone are unlikely to be sufficient to end intergenerational cycles of disadvantage.

Introduction

At the beginning of 2005, the number of children in poverty in Britain stood at around 3.5 million[1], which is around 28% of the child population. The fact that this many children live in relative financial hardship is a critical policy issue, and the government committed to reducing poverty rates by a quarter between 1998-99 and 2004-05, and to the more long-term goal of eradicating child poverty in the UK by 2020[2]. To help meet these targets, successive Labour governments have implemented a number of programmes to improve the incomes of families with children, including the Working Families Tax Credit and the Child Tax Credit.

This concern about child poverty relates not just to the immediate effects of the poverty experience. More importantly, the experience of poverty in childhood may influence social, economic and health outcomes throughout later life, leading to poverty in adulthood and consequences for the next generation. *This report explores the strength of the link between childhood poverty and poverty in later life, and asks whether this link has grown stronger or weaker for children growing up in the 1980s compared with children growing up in the 1970s.*

Childhood poverty is, however, clearly associated with other family attributes – such as low skills and health problems – that may be unfavourable to a child's progress and later economic success. Finding out whether childhood poverty is itself the real driver of subsequent adult poverty is vital for policy purposes. If it is, then improving the incomes of disadvantaged households may help break the intergenerational poverty cycle; but if other factors are the real cause then different policy interventions are needed. *While the research in this report is not aimed at precisely unpicking this causality, it does provide evidence on the contribution that family background characteristics make to the childhood–adulthood poverty link.*

There are numerous channels that could lead to a link between child and adult poverty. A shortage of material resources, low expectations or other psychological reactions could lead to low educational attainment, poor employability, lack of motivation, bad choices about the timing of childrearing and physical and mental health problems. All of these can engender poverty. *While this report can provide little evidence on the detailed mechanisms of poverty transmission, it does provide many insights into the contribution that educational, health, fertility and employment outcomes make towards the intergenerational persistence of poverty.*

The report examines in detail the magnitude of the link between child and adult poverty using members of two British cohorts, one group in their teens in the 1970s and the other in their teens in the 1980s (the National Child Development Study or NCDS and the British Cohort Study or BCS – see Box 1). The research shows to what extent this link is related to

---

[1] A child is counted as poor if they are in a family which has income after housing costs below 60% of the population median (Brewer at al, 2005).

[2] Information on the government's progress towards the child poverty reduction targets can be found in Brewer et al (2005). At the time of going to press, information on whether the 2004-05 target has been met is not yet available.

other family and individual characteristics and to what extent the link persists when we take account of these.

Earlier work has tackled similar themes using these two cohorts. That disadvantage persists along a number of different dimensions has been noted before in several research projects (Gregg and Machin, 1999; Bynner et al, 2002; Hobcraft, 2003, 2004), including some supported by the Joseph Rowntree Foundation. Gregg and Machin (1999) consider the impacts of growing up in disadvantage on a number of outcomes in later life for a group of children born in 1958. They find that children from socially disadvantaged backgrounds (characterised mainly by parental reports of financial hardship) have lower wages and are less likely to be in employment at the age of 33. Some, but not all, of this later disadvantage is driven by the fact that these children, on average, have lower educational attainments than those who do not experience disadvantage.

Part of the analysis in Bynner et al (2002, Chapter 6) also considers the later implications of disadvantage for the 1958 cohort, but adds analysis for a younger cohort born in 1970. This time disadvantage is measured in two ways: as having below average income and income that categorises the family as 'poor'. The authors find that poor children have lower educational attainment, more unemployment and lower earnings. The evidence suggests that the impact of poverty on these outcomes is larger in the second cohort than in the first.

The study by Bynner et al (2002) has a particular focus on the outcomes of young people, considering employment and earnings up to the mid-twenties. The research presented in our report uses the same datasets but includes much more recent information, enabling outcomes to be considered for more mature individuals, up to the age of 42 for the 1958 cohort and age 30 for the 1970 cohort. The focus is once again on the impact of early disadvantage on outcomes in later life, but in our case the main interest is on the connection between *poverty* in teens (at age 16) and *poverty* in adulthood. In general, the concern about employment, education and wages in previous studies are all driven by a concern with the connection between prior disadvantage and subsequent income (and by extension, material deprivation). This report looks at this connection directly, and then moves on to try and understand how the effects of teenage poverty on education, employment and family structure work together to lead to an increased risk of poverty in later life.

In summary, the questions we try to address in the following chapters are:

• How large is the transmission of poverty between a teenager's parents' circumstances and their own circumstances when they are in their early thirties?
• By how much has the strength of this transmission of poverty changed between the two cohorts that were in their teens in the 1970s and the 1980s?
• How far do other characteristics at the age of 16 and in adulthood explain these links?
• How far do the effects of early disadvantage continue to be felt as individuals reach middle age? (This can be considered by looking at outcomes at the age of 42.)

Our results find evidence of a significant persistence of poverty from teens to the early thirties and through to early middle age. Comparing the persistence of poverty from across the cohorts indicates that the strength of this persistence has approximately doubled.

No single factor can explain this increase. Differences in observable parental characteristics like education, employment, health, ethnic group and housing tenure can explain around half of the association between teenage and adult poverty. And certainly the role that these characteristics play in the transmission of poverty has increased between the decades studied. Yet a large proportion of the link between child and adult poverty cannot be put down to any parental characteristics that can be easily observed, other than low income, and the role this seems to play has doubled. *Financial resources in the teens seem to matter on top of any other driving background factors, and came to matter more between the 1970s and the 1980s.*

The organisation of the report

In Chapter 2 we discuss how poverty can be measured in the data, and document the extent of poverty in the cohorts under consideration. Following that, Chapter 3 shows the persistence of poverty across generations into early adulthood, and the way that it has changed between the cohorts. Chapter 4 considers to what extent this persists through to early middle age. Chapter 5 begins the process of understanding the mechanisms behind the persistence of poverty by documenting the relationship between poverty and other characteristics in both childhood and adulthood. In Chapter 6 we discuss the role that factors like education, employment, lone parenthood and ill health take in mediating the persistence of poverty into early adulthood and explore to what extent these explain the change in the persistence of poverty between 16 and adulthood. Finally, in Chapter 7, we consider the role of these mediating factors in poverty through to the age of 42. Chapter 8 summarises our findings.

Box 1: The British cohort studies

The data used in this research comes from the National Child Development Study and the British Cohort Study (referred to from now on as the NCDS and BCS). The NCDS includes all individuals born in a week in March 1958, while the BCS includes all individuals born in a week in April 1970. The main surveys that collected information about the NCDS cohort members were carried out at birth, ages 7, 11, 16, 33 and 42, while information on the second group of individuals was collected at birth, ages 5, 10, 16 and 30.

The adult income data used in this report is from the age 33 and 42 sweeps for the NCDS and the age 30 sweep for the BCS. In these sweeps the cohort members were asked to give details about all the sources of income received by themselves and any partner. In order to generate the poverty measures used, the income data was cleaned, adjusted to achieve comparability and finally adjusted for household composition. Further details on these processes and an evaluation of the quality of the final data used are found in the Appendix to this report.

Information used to characterise teenage poverty status in this report is obtained from the age 16 sweeps of the surveys where parents were asked to give details of their family income. This includes replies to questions on housing tenure, the presence of a father figure and the employment and education of parents. Similar variables relating to the cohort members are available from the adult sweeps, plus additional information about their partner (if any). The information on work histories taken in 1991 for the NCDS and 2000 for both cohorts provides data on the extent of individuals' work experience.

Figure 1 shows the NCDS and BCS cohorts on the same timeline, and shows the timing of the teenage and adulthood surveys used in this report. We refer to the cohort members at age 16 as teenagers, those at age 30 or 33 as in their thirties, and those at age 42 as middle aged, and generally distinguish between the cohorts by the decades they reached these ages, that is, the NCDS as teenagers in the 1970s and the BCS as in their early thirties in 2000.

Figure 1: Structure of the cohort studies

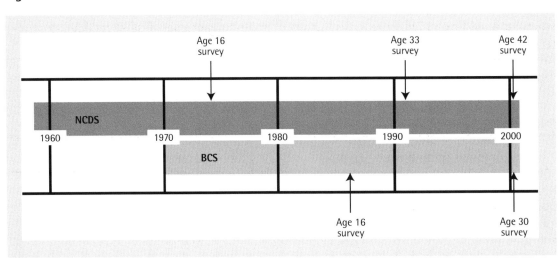

Measuring poverty

As outlined above, the information on poverty used in the key analysis is taken from parents when the cohort members were teenagers and from the cohort members themselves in their thirties and forties (the latter for the NCDS only). Our favoured definition of poverty[1] is a relative one, where families are defined as poor if their income – 'equivalised' by adjusting for household composition – falls below 60% of the median income in the population, before housing costs. Since the cohort studies are a particular subgroup of the population, the relevant poverty line in the population (in £ per week) must be derived from an alternative, nationally representative source, such as the Family Expenditure Survey (FES). Using this dataset we calculate the poverty lines in Britain[2] for the years of interest, and define those cohort members or parents with incomes below this line as those in poverty. We have also compared the proportions in poverty in our cohort datasets with the proportions of a similar age group that were in poverty in the nationally representative sample, and the numbers self-reporting financial hardship in the cohort surveys. The results of these comparisons are shown in the Appendix. The poverty rates based on the FES-derived poverty lines are shown in Table 1.

Using the FES poverty lines applied to the cohort studies, we find that 22% of teenagers lived in poverty with household income below £20.80 per week in the mid-1970s. This compares to 26% of teenagers in the mid-1980s with household incomes below £83.09 per week. This is substantially higher than the proportions in poverty in the FES using the same poverty lines, which are 14% in the mid-1970s and 16% in the mid-1980s (shown in the Appendix). This suggests some under-reporting of income in the cohort studies. Nevertheless, whatever measure we use suggests an increase of two to four percentage points in relative poverty for teenagers between the mid-1970s and mid-1980s, which is what we would expect given what is known about the general increase in income inequality over this period (see, for example, Gregg et al, 1999b or Brewer et al, 2005). The proportions of households self-reporting financial hardship in the cohort studies shows a similar increase – from 10% to 15% over the decade.

Table 1: Poverty rates in the cohort studies

	1974	1986	1991	2000
NCDS	Age 16		Age 33	Age 42
Men	22%		12%	12%
Women			19%	15%
BCS		Age 16		Age 30
Men		26%		9%
Women				12%

Note: Poverty line is defined as 60% of the population median of equivalised income.

---

[1] See Atkinson (1987) for a discussion of the various alternatives.

[2] The NCDS data includes a small number of observations from Northern Ireland, but excluding these does not change the results.

Moving into adulthood, we can see that the poverty rates for 30-year-olds at the beginning of the 1990s were higher than those of the same age group at the turn of the millennium – falling from 12% to 9% for men and 19% to 12% for women. There is clearly a big difference between genders: at all ages and in both cohorts women are between three and seven percentage points more likely to experience poverty than men and their poverty rates. This is surely attributable to their lower earnings, and the fact that they are more likely to be lone parents. By early middle age the differences between genders has lessened, but overall poverty was more prevalent among this age group than their younger contemporaries at the start of the 21st century.

The differences between poverty rates based on alternative definitions are much smaller for adult cohort members than they are in the teens. This is likely to be because the method of obtaining income information for the adult cohort members is much more similar to the questions used in the FES, in that individuals are asked detailed questions about the different components of income.

Key points

Teenage poverty increased between the mid-1970s and mid-1980s. At the turn of the 21st century, 12% of men who were teenagers in the mid-1970s and 9% of men who were teenagers in the mid-1980s were in poverty. The poverty rate among women of the same generation was three percentage points higher.

The persistence of poverty from childhood to adulthood

The link between teenage and adult poverty

Having defined poverty and shown the proportions in poverty at each stage in the lifecycle, we can now examine the link between individuals' poverty experiences at these different points in time. Table 2 breaks down the percentage of men and women experiencing poverty in adulthood according to whether they were poor as teenagers. Comparing the proportions in poverty, it is immediately clear that there is a persistence of poverty across the generations between these time periods. Those men and women who were in poor households as teenagers are much more likely to be poor as adults in their thirties. For example, 19% of men who experienced poverty as teenagers in the 1970s were in poverty in their thirties, compared with only 10% of those who were not poor in their teens.

Table 2: The relationship between poverty in teens and adulthood

	Poor as teenagers		Not poor as teenagers	
	Poor in their thirties (%)	Not poor in their thirties (%)	Poor in their thirties (%)	Not poor in their thirties (%)
Teenage boys in the mid-1970s	18.9	81.2	10.1	89.9
Teenage boys in the mid-1980s	18.6	81.5	5.3	94.7
Teenage girls in the mid-1970s	28.8	71.2	16.9	83.1
Teenage girls in the mid-1980s	23.7	76.3	8.0	92.0

Note: The table reports percentages poor at the age of 30 by childhood poverty status, and odds ratios and their *t*-statistics. Figures are based on 2,272 men and 2,243 women from the NCDS and 2,133 men and 2,403 women from the BCS.

The next challenge is to find a clear way to compare the persistence in poverty between the two cohorts and across the genders. In order to do this we require a measure that is insensitive to differences in poverty rates between genders and to changes in poverty rates over time. The measure we use is the *odds ratio* (see Box 2). We will use this odds ratio – which describes the extent to which being brought up in poverty increases the likelihood of being poor rather than non-poor – as our central index of the persistence of poverty across generations. An odds ratio of 1 means that there is no association between being poor as a teenager and being poor in adulthood. An odds ratio of 2 means that being poor as a teenager doubles the odds of being poor as an adult.

Box 2: Measuring persistence using odds ratios

It is important to understand the concept of the *odds ratio* as it is used throughout the analysis that follows. In Table 2 it can be seen that, for NCDS sons with poor parents, the *odds* of being poor are 18.9%/81.2% or 0.232 to 1. This means you are 4.3 times more likely to be non-poor than poor if your family was poor when you were 16. These odds can also be calculated for those whose parents are not poor. In this case the odds of being poor are 0.112 to 1, so individuals are 8.9 times more likely to be non-poor than poor if their parents were non-poor.

To calculate the effect that poverty in childhood has on the chances of being poor as an adult we simply divide these two odds to find the *odds ratio*, which in this case is 0.232/0.112 = 2.069[1]. This is the summary measure of the persistence of poverty used in much of our analysis. If the chances of poverty at the age of 33 are unaffected by poverty at 16 the odds ratio would be 1. In the case where the relationship between the two variables is reversed, so that poverty at 16 leads to a reduced chance of poverty at 33, the odds ratio would be less than 1.

The odds ratio can be easily derived using multivariate logit regression models. This, in turn, makes it straightforward to also control for the influences of additional factors that may explain why the probability of being poor is linked across time periods. The variables representing those influences are included as explanatory variables in the model.

Table 3 presents these indices, which have been derived from Table 2. It is clear from this that our index of the persistence of poverty is similar for men and women who were teenagers in the 1970, with an odds ratio of around 2 in each case. It is also evident that there has been a strong rise in the persistence of poverty between these teenagers and teenagers in the 1980s, with much higher odds ratios in the second column in Table 3. The last column shows the change in the odds ratio. This change is particularly large for men, for whom the odds ratio doubles from 2 to 4.

These odds ratios and the difference in the odds ratios are all statistically significant at conventional levels. By this we mean that we can have a high degree of confidence that the poverty odds ratios in the population that these samples come from are different from 1, and that the difference between the odds ratios for the different cohorts is not 0.

To help visualise the magnitude of these changes, see Figure 2. We will see later how taking account of other family and individual characteristics changes the picture.

Table 3: Indicators of the persistence of poverty from teens to adulthood

	Odds ratios for association of teenage poverty with poverty in adulthood (age 30–33)		
	Teenagers in mid-1970s	Teenagers in mid-1980s	Difference between cohorts
Men	2.07	4.00	1.93
Women	2.00	3.56	1.56

Note: All odds ratios statistically significant at any measurable level.

Differences in odds ratios statistically significant at 1% level.

Figures based on 2,272 men and 2,243 women from the NCDS and 2,133 men and 2,403 women from the BCS.

---

[1] A further explanation of the odds ratio is found in Heath (1981, pp 261-2).

Figure 2: How teenage poverty affects the odds of being poor as an adult

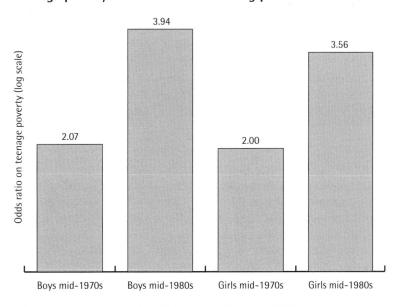

Note: The bars report the odds ratios for poverty at age 16 in a model of poverty at 33/30, as shown in Table 3. Vertical scale is in logarithms.

So, disadvantage became more persistent across generations for the more recent cohort, a finding that should add to the government's determination to reduce child poverty and adopt additional policies to ameliorate childhood disadvantage. This finding is not unexpected given the analysis in Blanden et al (2004), which finds an increased relationship between parental income and children's own later earnings and family earnings. This research also found a particularly strong increase for men. Many commentators have inferred from this that the impact on adult poverty from poverty in childhood will be greater in the later cohort. The results presented here show this explicitly[2].

Before we continue, there are a couple of comments to be made about the interpretation of the odds ratios we have found. For both cohorts, we find significant persistence in the extent of poverty. However, it is also clear from the numbers discussed in Box 2 that even among those who have poor parents the chances of being poor are low. This may lead some readers to regard the persistence of poverty as being quite weak. It must be remembered, however, that the point-in-time poverty measures we are using are likely to have some measurement error, and will also reflect transitory variations in poverty. For both these reasons, the odds ratios observed are likely to be lower bounds on the true extent of the persistence of poverty (see Freeman, 1984, for more discussion of the consequences of misclassification error). When comparing across the cohorts, what is important is that measurement error has similar implications in both cohorts, an issue spoken to in the discussion of the quality of the data in the Appendix.

In order to check the robustness of our findings, we experiment with other measures of poverty, and the results of this exercise are shown in Table 4. For simplicity, we report only the odds ratios and the change in these from one cohort to the next, alongside indicators of the statistical reliability of the results (as described for Table 3). In all cases there is a substantial increase in persistence, with all the figures in the 'Change' column being greater than 0. However, it does appear that we measure the strongest rise in persistence when the FES poverty lines are used to define poverty. In the majority of cases (5 out of 8) we can be

---

2   We have attempted to detect regional differences in persistence, but even when regions are defined as countries the sample sizes do not show any statistically significant differences, although there is limited evidence that the increases in persistence have been particularly strong in England and Wales compared with Scotland.

confident that the persistence of poverty has increased between the cohorts (the *p*-values that indicate the probability of there really being no change are less than 5%). The only result that is substantially below the statistical standard for confidence in the results is that derived from parental reports of financial difficulties for female cohort members. This is because the persistence in poverty measured using this index is stronger for the cohort who were teenagers in the mid-1970s than for any other definition. It is, however, hard to know what to infer from this since we are not entirely sure what leads parents to define themselves as in financial difficulties.

One concern about the data from the cohort studies is the extent to which attrition of respondents from the studies and non-response to particular questions influences the conclusions drawn. An extensive investigation of these issues suggests that these factors do not have a strong influence on our findings (see Box 3).

Table 4: Measures of the persistence of poverty from teens to adulthood based on alternative poverty definitions

Measures of poverty used		Odds ratios for effect of teenage poverty on adult poverty		
Teens	Adulthood	Mid–1970s teenagers	Mid–1980s teenagers	Change
Men				
FES poverty line	FES poverty line	2.07	3.94	1.88
FES proportion in poverty	FES proportion in poverty	2.41	3.38	0.97
FES proportion in poverty	FES poverty line	2.09	3.76	1.68
Parent self-reported financial difficulties	FES poverty line	2.39 / 2,826	3.55 / 2,654	*1.60*
Women				
FES poverty line	FES poverty line	2.00	3.56	1.56
FES proportion in poverty	FES proportion in poverty	2.10	3.08	0.98
FES proportion in poverty	FES poverty line	2.05	3.53	1.48
Parent self-reported financial difficulties	FES poverty line	2.30 / 2,805	2.80 / 3,027	0.50

Notes:

Bold: less than 5% chance of no real difference between the groups in the population.

Italics: less than 10% chance of no real difference between the groups in the population.

Normal: more than 10% chance of no real difference between the groups in the population.

Sample sizes: mid-1970s 2,272 teenage boys, 2,132 girls; mid-1980s 2,243 teenage boys, 2,403 girls, except for rows based on self-reported financial difficulties: corresponding numbers 2,826, 2,654, 2,805, 3,027.

Descriptive statistics for these measures are included in Appendix, Table A11.

Box 3: Attrition and item non-response in the cohort studies

The NCDS and BCS cohorts began with a sample of around 17,000 to 18,000 each. In Table 2, just 5,000 individuals are used from each cohort; individuals are lost from the samples both because they cease to be included in the surveys (attrition) and because they do not answer key questions (non-response). Non-response is unfortunately a particular difficulty with income questions. It might be that the individuals used in our samples do not show the same picture of poverty persistence that would be observed in the full population. In the worst case scenario, it could be that the impact of this selection is different in each cohort, meaning that the change in poverty persistence observed is solely the consequence of data problems and not real changes in the underlying patterns of persistence.

In order to examine these issues we have conducted an extensive analysis of the patterns of attrition and non-response in the two cohorts (the results are shown in Tables A3-A7 in the Appendix). In general the findings are reassuring although there is evidence that disadvantaged groups are slightly less likely to be included in the final sample, and that this effect is slightly stronger in the second cohort.

As a check on the impact of attrition and non-response we used a number of characteristics to predict which individuals drop out of the sample after the age of 16[3]. The models can be used to predict the probability of remaining in the survey and these predictions used to weight the data accordingly, giving more weight to the types of individuals who are under-represented. Despite using a number of variables that should be related to response rates and attrition (proportion of questions answered in previous surveys, number of home moves, social class etc) it was very difficult to find the causes of drop-out. This indicates that there is not a consistent pattern of drop-out, which is encouraging. Consequently re-weighting the sample makes almost no difference to the results. The results of the drop out equations and re-weighting are presented in Tables A8-A10 in the Appendix.

The link with poverty in earlier childhood

So far our results have focused on the persistence of poverty between teens (age 16) and adulthood (age 33/30). Using the later BCS cohort, we can look further at patterns of persistence relating to childhood poverty at an earlier age, because the study also records parents' income when the child was 10 years old. The results of this exercise are interesting. While poverty as a teenager and poverty at age 10 both have a strong relationship with poverty in adulthood, the relationship with teenage poverty is rather stronger than that with earlier childhood poverty. If we look at the link between poverty experienced at age 10 and adult poverty, we calculate odds ratios of 2.7 for both genders, compared with the 4 and 3.5 shown in Figure 2 for teenage poverty. If we measure the effect of poverty at each age after taking account of the effect of poverty at the other age, the odds ratios on both fall – but *teenage poverty is much more important in determining poverty in adulthood than poverty in earlier childhood*. Taking this at face value, poverty during the late teenage years on which our main study focuses seems critical.

Another question is whether the effect of poverty in earlier childhood and in teens just 'add up' in terms of their influence on adult poverty, or whether there is an additional effect from an experience of persistent poverty in childhood. We find, perhaps surprisingly, that the effects of poverty at these two childhood ages do simply add up. This in itself might suggest that the effect of poverty we are measuring is not simply due to underlying characteristics. To see this, consider that we detect three types of child poverty: a group in

---

[3] To be included in these models, individuals must be in the survey up to the age of 16 otherwise there would be very few variables available to use to predict their later behaviour. Drop-out occurs either because there is no valid income report for parents and children or because they drop out of the survey altogether after the age of 16.

poverty when the child is 10, a group in poverty when the child is 16, and a group in poverty in both periods. It seems plausible that a loss of resources as a child and a loss of resources as a teenager result in a larger loss of resources and a proportionately larger effect on poverty as an adult. However, we would also expect families prone to persistent or repeat spells in poverty to be qualitatively different from those experiencing transient poverty (in terms of innate abilities, skill levels, motivation or health), and there is no reason to expect such an adding up condition to apply if it is these underlying characteristics that drive the intergenerational transmission of poverty.

Key points

Being poor as a teenager has a strong bearing on the chances of being poor as an adult. Being poor as a teenager in the 1970s doubled the odds of a person being poor in their thirties in 1991. The prospects for poor teenagers worsened between the 1970s and the 1980s. Being poor as a teenager in the 1980s nearly quadrupled the odds of being poor as a 30-year-old in 2000.

4

The persistence of poverty from teens to middle age

The main results from the previous chapter indicate that poverty persisted among the members of the 1958 cohort who were teenagers in the mid-1970s: being poor as a teenager doubled the odds of being poor as an adult at age 33. Recent data, obtained from the same NCDS cohort members in 2000, allows us to continue the examination of the persistence of poverty through to age 42 when the cohort was entering middle age.

As we are now considering the relationship between three outcomes, poverty as a teenager (16), as an adult (33) and in middle age (42), it is necessary to be a little more creative in the way that the results are described and presented. The way we do this is to calculate the proportions of the cohort who experience various combinations of poverty outcomes over the three periods. These combinations and the proportions we observe in each group are shown in the first column of Table 5 below. Just 1.4% of the men in the sample are poor in all three periods, while almost 70% are not experiencing poverty at any of the survey dates. Some 3.6% of boys who were poor as teenagers grew up to experience poverty, either as an adult at age 30, or in middle age.

These figures are not helpful on their own. To understand what they mean, it is necessary to compare them with what we would expect if poverty were not persistent, such that an individual's likelihood of experiencing poverty if one period was completely unrelated to their experience in other periods. This is done in the second column of Table 5. The proportions here are the proportion with each combination of outcomes if poverty in each period were independent, that is, what we would find if there was no persistence. From these it is clear that *although just 1.4% of the men in the sample are poor in all periods, this is actually extremely high compared with the proportion we would expect to see without any persistence, which is 0.19%.* In the third column, we state whether the difference between the actual and expected proportion is positive or negative and whether it is significant in the statistical sense (that is, we can be confident that the proportions in the population are different from what we would observe if there was no persistence).

Once again, there is strong evidence of the persistence of poverty, both across generations and between early adulthood and middle age. The proportions are higher than expected without persistence, both when individuals are poor in all periods and when they are non-poor in all periods. In addition, there appears to be persistence between the thirties and middle age that is unrelated to poverty status as a teenager. We can see this because more people are poor in both their thirties and forties than would be the case if being poor in middle age was unrelated to being poor as a younger adult, even amongst those who are not poor as teenagers.

Table 5, therefore, gives an explicit summary of how poverty is related over three periods. There are two ways to break this persistence down in order to understand it more completely; the way this is done depends on what is considered as the outcome of interest. There are two alternatives here.

Table 5: Proportions with a combination of poverty outcomes at ages 16, 33 and 42

Men	Observed percentage	Expected percentage without persistence	Implication for persistence of poverty
Poor in all periods	1.40	0.19	Persistent
Poor in no periods	69.60	65.39	Persistent
Poor in teens then not poor in adulthood	14.83	16.16	Not significant
Not poor in teens then poor in both adult surveys	2.43	0.75	Persistent
Poor in teens then poor in one adult survey	3.59	3.47	Not significant
Not poor in teens then poor in one adult survey	8.15	14.04	Persistent

Women	Observed percentage	Expected percentage without persistence	Implication for persistence of poverty
Poor in all periods	3.12	0.59	Persistent
Poor in no periods	60.38	54.32	Persistent
Poor in teens then not poor in adulthood	14.47	15.35	Not significant
Not poor in teens then poor in both adult surveys	4.74	2.09	Persistent
Poor in teens then poor in one adult survey	4.44	6.09	Not significant
Not poor in teens then poor in one adult survey	12.85	21.55	Persistent

Note: These results are based on the FES poverty line definition of poverty but are extremely robust to other definitions.

The first is to consider middle age poverty as the outcome, and think about how teenage and earlier adulthood poverty influences this. This allows easy comparison of the persistence of poverty through to middle age with the results for early adulthood shown in the previous chapters. We saw before that teenage poverty doubled the odds of being poor for the cohort we are considering here. Similarly, being poor as a teenager in the 1970s doubled the odds of being poor in early middle age at the beginning of the millennium. So, we see that teenage poverty is as strongly related to middle age poverty as it was to poverty in earlier adulthood.

To some extent, this is surprising because we might expect that the longer the time period between measures, the more the influence of teenage poverty should have faded. One explanation for the result we find could be that teenage poverty influences poverty in early adulthood, and that this then links through to poverty in later life. In other words, there may be no direct link from teenage poverty to middle age once we take account of whether or not a person is poor in their thirties. We can see to what extent this is true by looking at the direct influence of teenage poverty on middle age poverty after taking account of whether an individual is poor in their thirties (and, similarly, measuring the effect of poverty in their thirties after taking account of whether they were poor as a teenager).

The second column of Table 6 shows the odds ratios derived from this approach[1]. Firstly, it is clear that a person experiencing poverty in their thirties has much higher odds of being poor in middle age than someone who is not poor in their thirties. In fact, the odds of being poor are increased eight-fold. There is clearly a very important link between poverty across time periods for adults and one that is much stronger than the link between poverty

---

[1] This is based on a logit regression model.

from teens to adulthood (see Jarvis and Jenkins, 1997, for a detailed look at links between low income in different periods for adults). However, the larger link for poverty from between 33 and 42 compared with 16 and adulthood it not surprising when we remember that poverty at 33 and 42 is in both cases a consequence of the cohort members' characteristics while poverty at age 16 is a consequence of parents' characteristics.

So the link between poverty in early adulthood and middle age does explain part of the link from teenage poverty to middle age poverty, but it does not explain much of it: being poor as a teenager increases the odds of being poor in early middle age by a factor of around 1.7-1.8 even allowing for differences in poverty in a person's thirties. In other words, teenage poverty is associated with poverty through to middle age regardless of whether a person was poor in their thirties or not. The third column adds a variable describing whether the individual was poor as a teenager and poor in the early thirties. This is similar to the analysis of poverty at age 10 and 16, and has the same result. The impact of poverty at age 16 is similar whether the individual is poor in their early thirties or not; there is no evidence that being poor in more than one survey raises the chances of being poor later in life more than would be expected from combining the impacts of being poor in each period.

Table 6: The persistence of poverty through to middle age

	Odd ratios for effect on middle age poverty (age 42)	Odds ratios for effect on middle age poverty (age 42)	Odds ratios for effect on middle age poverty (age 42)
Boys poor in mid-1970s	2.00	1.67	1.93
... as men in their thirties		8.80	10.20
Poor as teenagers and in thirties			0.63
Girls poor in mid-1970s	2.13	1.80	1.61
... as women in their thirties		7.97	7.41
Poor as teenagers and in thirties			1.27

Notes: Numbers reported are the odds ratios for being poor in the stated survey in a model of poverty at 42. Poverty in all periods is defined on the basis of the FES poverty line. The second column reports the effect of poverty at age 16 (or 33) conditional on poverty at age 33 (or 16).
Bold: less than 1% chance of no real difference between the groups in the population.
Normal: more than 10% chance of no real difference between the groups in the population.
Sample sizes: column 1 men, 2,357, women 2,377; columns 2 and 3 men, 1,645, women 1,666.

Another way of looking at this is to place individuals into three groups, ranked according to the severity of their experience of poverty in adulthood and middle age, and to model the influence of teenage poverty on an individual's position in this ranking. Here we define three ranked outcomes based on the surveys at age 33 and 42: (1) not poor in thirties or middle age; (2) poor in one or other of these age periods; and (3) poor in both thirties and middle age. Using these categories we can estimate odds ratios using a model that is appropriate for ranked outcomes[2]. In this case, the interpretation of the odds ratio is that it shows the extent to which childhood poverty increases the odds of being in one ranked outcome category rather than the one below it. Table 7 shows these results. Again, for both men and women the odds ratios are close to two. Being poor in childhood doubles the odds of a person being poor at one or other adult survey relative to being poor at neither

---

[2] An ordered logit model.

Table 7: Effect of teenage poverty on ranked adult/middle age poverty outcomes

	Odds ratios for poverty in adult surveys: (1) not poor in both; (2) poor in one or other; (3) poor in both	
	Men	Women
Teenager poor in mid-1970s	2.23	1.89

Note: All odds ratios are statistically significant at 1% level or better.

(Category 2 relative to Category 1) and doubles the odds of being poor at both surveys relative to being poor at one or the other (Category 3 relative to Category 2). By implication, this means that teenage poverty quadrupled the odds of being poor in both thirties and middle age rather than not being poor at either of these ages. Although the estimates of the effect of teenage poverty seem stronger for men than for women, the difference is not important statistically.

Key points

The link between poverty in teens and adulthood continues to have a bearing through to middle age, regardless of whether or not a person is recorded as poor in their thirties. Being poor as a teenager nearly doubles the odds of being poor in early middle age or early thirties, and quadruples the odds of being recorded in poverty in middle age *and* earlier adulthood.

5

Poverty and disadvantage in childhood and adulthood

The results so far have measured the strength of the associations between the persistence of poverty at different ages; the next step is to attempt to understand more about what other factors are associated with the persistence of poverty over the lifecycle.

First, it should be noted that it is extremely difficult to pin down the factors that *cause* the persistence of poverty. Monetary poverty goes hand-in-hand with numerous other forms of deprivation, some of which are consequences of the lack of resources in the household and others that in themselves lead to poverty. Many of these aspects of deprivation may be a result of other underlying factors that are very hard to measure, and that may themselves persist through individuals' lives. For all these reasons, it is extremely difficult to really understand the causal processes that lie at the route of the persistence of poverty through the lifecycle.

What we can do is to document the links between poverty and deprivation at particular ages and then to demonstrate how these are associated across different points in the lifecycle. This will provide evidence on the dominant characteristics that are associated with the persistence of poverty and disadvantage over time.

The characteristics of the families of those who are poor as teenagers

Table 8 provides evidence on the characteristics that are associated with poverty in the two cohorts when the individuals were teenagers. When considering these, we have attempted to take account of many of the important routes that we believe are likely to lead from disadvantage in childhood to disadvantage later in life. These are demographic characteristics (being brought up by a lone mother at the age of 16, coming from a large family, being from a non-white ethnic group), housing and neighbourhood conditions (proxied by accommodation in social housing), the child's own ill health (which is considered as an explicit antecedent to later health difficulties) and parental employment and low education. To reiterate, we are *not* proposing these as factors that cause childhood poverty, but as factors that are associated with child poverty and that may exert a direct influence on poverty in adulthood.

The first two columns of Table 8 show the percentages with the characteristic in the poor and non-poor groups, while (in keeping with the rest of the analysis) the third column shows the relationship between poverty and the characteristics expressed as an odds ratio. In the final column, we report the odds ratios from a 'conditional' model of poverty. These show the association between each characteristic and poverty, holding the other factors constant; more will be said about this below. It is clear from the first three columns that

Table 8: The link between key aspects of family disadvantage and teenage poverty

| | | Association with teenage poverty | | |
	Proportions in each category	Proportions in each category	Characteristics separately (unconditional)	Characteristics together (conditional)
Characteristics of household	Poor	Non-poor	Odds ratios	Odds ratios
Teenagers in 1970s				
No father in household	17%	5%	4.09	**10.50**
Average number of children	2.9	1.5	**1.82**	**1.86**
Non-white	4%	3%	1.49	0.82
Social housing	60%	37%	**2.59**	**1.43**
Month+ ill in school year	9%	5%	**1.85**	1.24
Father not working	18%	3%	**7.75**	**5.77**
Mother not working	65%	24%	**5.84**	**5.96**
Neither parent working	14%	1%	**16.71**	1.39
Father minimum school age	83%	70%	**2.13**	**1.74**
Mother minimum school age	82%	68%	**2.17**	**1.30**
Teenagers in 1980s				
No father in household	13%	6%	**2.43**	**3.18**
Average number of children	2.2	1.8	**1.44**	**1.31**
Non-white	7%	2%	**3.50**	**2.91**
Social housing	44%	9%	**8.45**	**4.08**
Month+ ill in school year	5%	3%	**1.84**	1.29
Father not working	42%	4%	**17.75**	**8.86**
Mother not working	55%	18%	**5.45**	**3.09**
Neither parent working	33%	2%	**21.84**	1.16
Father minimum school age	83%	62%	**2.96**	**2.23**
Mother minimum school age	86%	64%	**3.76**	**1.63**

Notes: Household defined as poor if household income is below poverty line derived from FES.

'Month+ ill in school year' is a combination of two variables: not only do parents need to report the child as having taken a month off ill, but they must also state that the child has seen their GP during the year.

Unconditional odds ratios report the odds ratio between poverty at 16 and the characteristic. Conditional odds ratios report the odds ratio between poverty at 16 and the characteristic in a multivariate model with all the other characteristics also included.

Bold: less than 5% chance of no real difference between the groups in the population.

Sample sizes: 8,856 NCDS, 7,127 BCS.

there are associations between poverty and the chosen measures of disadvantage in both cohorts. Children in poorer households are more likely to lack a father figure, have more siblings, be non-white, live in social housing and take time off school due to ill health, all of which are consistent with previous research on poverty (Gregg et al, 1999b). Unsurprisingly, perhaps, it is also the case that their parents are less likely to work and more likely to have a lower standard of education. In all cases, the differences in these characteristics between poor and non-poor children are significant.

There have been, however, some interesting and important changes in the cohorts over time. In terms of the first two measures, the association between poverty and living with a lone mother and the number of children in the household has declined between the cohorts. These are likely to be a consequence of general demographic changes, such as the rise in the number of lone parents and the increase in the age when older children tend to leave home, among others. For all the other outcomes (except for missing school through illness) the associations between poverty and deprivation have risen. There are clear explanations for many of these changes. The strong increase in the association between poverty and social housing is a consequence of the selling off of council houses between the time when the first cohort was surveyed in 1974, and 1986 when the second cohort was 16, creating a concentration of the poorest in the social housing that remained. There was a strong rise in the correlation between poverty and both father's unemployment and having no one working in the household, showing that the poor are much more likely to lack employment in the second cohort. This is in line with the rise in workless households over this period discussed in Gregg et al (1999a). In addition, the increasing relationship between poverty and parental low educational attainment is in line with the rising returns to education over this period.

The numbers reported in the final column of the table reveal how each characteristic is associated with poverty after we take account of the other characteristics of disadvantage. These 'conditional' models help us to understand if the correlations between poverty and, say, ethnicity, are driven by the other aspects of disadvantage – for example, because non-white families have poorer education or are less likely to be employed[1]. In Table 8, the odds ratios that remain statistically significant are reported in bold. For almost every family characteristic, the odds ratio that shows its relationship with teenage poverty is reduced once the other family factors are taken into account. However, most remain individually important and statistically significant. There are some exceptions: teenagers in non-white families in the mid-1970s tended to be poor, but only because these families were less likely to be employed and more likely to have lower education than their non-white counterparts. Similarly, teenagers in the 1970s and 1980s who had more than one month off school in a year tended to be in poor families, but as we might expect, the poverty was really linked to other family factors and not the time taken off school. Note that even in these 'conditional' estimates, non-employment and low education have a much stronger link with poverty in the second cohort than the first: teenagers in the 1980s with a father employed had much lower odds of being poor than did the teenagers with a father employed in the 1970s; teenagers with low-educated parents had much higher odds of being in poverty in the 1980s than the 1970s. Overall, around 33% of the variance in teenage poverty is linked to the set of family characteristics listed in Table 8.

The characteristics of poor adults

Table 9 takes a similar approach to understanding poverty and disadvantage for our cohorts in early adulthood. The aim here is to consider similar characteristics to those related to teenage poverty in the previous chapter: whether the cohort member has a partner, the number of children in the household, lone-parent status, ethnicity, social housing, whether the individual has a limiting health condition and the employment status and education level of the cohort member and any partner. Additionally, to add a lifecycle aspect, we include information on the proportion of time spent in full-time employment from the age of 16 to the survey date (excluding time in full-time education from the denominator, so that those with higher education do not appear to have weaker labour market attachment). For adults, there are important differences by gender that need to be illustrated, so we save space in the table by listing the odds ratios only.

Many of the associations between disadvantage and poverty are similar across the two cohorts. The differences between genders are more noticeable, with poor health more strongly related to poverty among men, while women without a partner run a relatively

---

[1] We run a logit model of poverty on all the other characteristics.

higher risk of living in poverty[2]. This reflects the fact that men are still likely to earn the majority of household income, so their own education and employment is most important for men, while partners' characteristics are more important for women. On this point, there is evidence of a change over the 1990s, with women in 2000 more reliant on their own employment to avoid poverty. In contrast, results for work experience show that, if anything, this is more important to women in the early 1990s than those in 2000 – this may be picking up a stronger relationship in the earlier cohort between weak labour market attachment for women in their twenties, lone parenthood and poverty.

As before, we also report the conditional correlations once all characteristics are taken into account together. These show the association between the characteristic and poverty, holding all the other characteristics constant. The most striking feature of these results is the central role of employment in governing poverty status: both employment at the survey date and employment history are strongly significant. Being out of work increases the odds of being poor 78-fold for men. For women, partner's employment status is more important than their own. It is also clear that a limiting health difficulty is only associated with poverty to the extent that it results in a person being out of work. For men in the early 1990s with the same employment status, a limiting health problem actually significantly reduces the probability of being poor. A person's education and that of their partner matter too, over and above employment status, with low education almost doubling the odds of being poor, although this has much become less important for adult women over the decade between 1991 and 2000[3].

Accommodation in social housing is strongly associated with poverty in all models despite the inclusion of the other variables. This may mean that it is picking up an aspect of deprivation not captured in the other variables, but it may just reflect that the poorest tend to be socially housed irrespective of their other characteristics. The interpretation of social housing is somewhat problematic in all these models, because it is the variable that is most clearly a consequence of poverty rather than a cause. In the later analysis we check the robustness of the results to the inclusion or exclusion of this variable.

Overall, the mediators of poverty in adulthood listed in Table 9 explain about 55% of the variance in poverty across these households, although somewhat less than this for women in their thirties in 2000 (about 45%).

To complete the picture of poverty and disadvantage, we now consider which characteristics seem to be responsible for mediating poverty in early middle age (42). In general, similar factors are important in middle age as were important in a person's early thirties. There are some exceptions. The number of children becomes less relevant as individuals age, probably because better-off couples are more likely to have children later in life[4]. There is a weaker relationship between poverty and living in social housing, perhaps because housing tenure is more strongly related to previous circumstances rather than current needs as people age. Once again employment and education are driving factors that operate over and above the others in the conditional model. It is notable that men's

---

[2] The results shown here do not draw out the differences in means across the cohorts, for example, fewer individuals are in partnerships in the second cohort compared with the first. Rather they show the relative differences between poor and non-poor in the two cohorts.

[3] Note, however, that we are accounting for residence in social housing in these models; in fact if we exclude social housing from our models, a partner's education has a significant influence on poverty. In other words, women with low-educated partners in 2000 tend to be poor and in social housing.

[4] *Birth Statistics* (ONS, 2004, Table 11.4) shows the rise in the mother's age at first birth for births in marriage by father's socio-economic group. This varies from almost 32 for those with professional husbands to 28 for those with husbands in routine occupations.

Table 9: The links between adulthood characteristics and household poverty

	Men aged 33 in 1991		Men aged 30 in 2000	
	Characteristics separately	Characteristics together	Characteristics separately	Characteristics together
Single	1.76	1.71	1.39	3.35
Number of children in household	4.15	1.78	4.22	1.72
Lone parent	1.46	0.36	1.76	1.88
Non-white	1.80	1.66	1.80	1.66
Council tenant	10.34	2.96	7.50	1.77
Limiting health condition	3.47	0.48	3.18	0.68
Cohort member not working	63.07	40.59	61.01	78.02
Partner not working	10.96	6.04	19.57	13.59
No one working	82.45	1.98	73.28	1.12
Proportion of time in employment	0.01	0.33	0.03	1.11
Low education cohort member	4.32	1.98	3.55	1.93
Low education partner	3.81	1.88	3.66	1.84
	Women aged 33 in 1991		Women aged 30 in 2000	
	Characteristics separately	Characteristics together	Characteristics separately	Characteristics together
Single	2.43	0.22	2.24	2.16
Number of children in household	7.94	1.75	5.85	1.45
Lone parent	1.94	1.55	2.32	0.70
Non-white	2.15	2.30	1.71	1.41
Council tenant	8.45	1.65	8.89	1.76
Limiting health condition	1.57	0.74	1.83	0.59
Cohort member not working	7.61	4.66	18.22	7.98
Partner not working	51.88	53.63	31.66	19.51
No one working	54.48	1.77	29.20	1.09
Proportion of time in employment	0.02	0.11	0.02	0.14
Low education cohort member	4.24	1.68	2.90	0.98
Low education partner	4.10	2.87	2.95	1.43

Notes: Low education is defined for the cohort member as not obtaining some O levels or equivalent, for the cohort member's partner it is defined as leaving school at age 16.

Unconditional odds ratios report the odds ratio between poverty at 33/30 and the characteristic. Conditional odds ratios report the odds ratio between poverty at 33/30 and the characteristic in a multivariate model with all the other characteristics also included.

Bold: less than 5% chance of no real difference between the groups in the population.

Sample sizes: 1991: men 3,906, women 3,842; 2000: men 4,315, women 4,644.

previous employment experience has relatively weak independent effects on household poverty, once current employment status and other attributes are taken into account. For women, however, recent work history is important. Overall, these attributes account for about 43% of the variance in poverty across households in middle age.

Table 10: The links between middle age characteristics and household poverty

	Men		Women	
	Characteristics separately	Characteristics together	Characteristics separately	Characteristics together
Single	2.06	2.18	2.90	0.22
Number of children in household	1.26	2.00	4.28	1.82
Lone parent	2.95	0.90	1.39	0.74
Non-white	1.77	1.80	1.45	0.82
Council tenant	4.17	1.33	5.92	1.92
Limiting health condition	3.68	0.60	2.45	0.91
Cohort member not working	27.69	27.80	8.03	4.43
Partner not working	8.14	5.43	31.04	31.99
No one working	31.56	1.12	22.56	0.93
Proportion of time in full-time employment up to 33	0.05	0.74	0.10	0.70
Proportion of time in full-time employment 33-42	0.04	0.63	0.10	0.20
Low education cohort member	2.82	1.80	2.85	1.60
Low education partner	2.81	2.43	4.93	3.07

Notes: Unconditional odds ratios report the odds ratio between poverty at 42 and the characteristic. Conditional odds ratios report the odds ratio between poverty at 42 and the characteristic in a multivariate model with all the other characteristics also included.

Bold: less than 5% chance of no real difference between the groups in the population.

Sample sizes: men: 4,026, women: 4,127.

Key points

In the mid-1970s teenagers in poverty tended to be white children in large families, with a low-educated father or mother, at least one of whom was not working. Living with a lone mother in the household was especially strongly linked to teenage poverty. By the mid-1980s, low education, paternal non-employment and being non-white were more strongly linked to teenage poverty, but being brought up by a lone mother was less relevant. Similar factors come into play in adulthood household poverty, and there are few differences between the early 1990s and the start of the new millennium. Unsurprisingly, being out of work, having a partner out of work or having little accumulated work history are the factors most closely associated with poverty now – both for adults in middle age and in their thirties – although low education also plays an important role.

6

Explaining the persistence of poverty and its change over time

The role of family background characteristics and adult outcomes

The preceding analysis sheds substantial light on the important factors that are correlated with poverty at the different points in the lifecycle. The next task – and one central to our analysis – is to gauge the extent to which these factors might explain the links between poverty in childhood and poverty in adulthood. There are four key questions:

- Is it teenage poverty that leads to poverty in later life, or is it those other family characteristics that we showed are linked to teenage poverty that really matter – like parental low education and non-employment?
- Do teenage poverty and other aspects of teenage disadvantage lead to poverty only through the main adult mediators we identified – education and employment – or are there more complex processes at work?
- Is the rise we observe in the influence of teenage poverty between the 1970s and 1980s due to changes in the relationship between childhood family characteristics and teenage poverty?
- Has teenage poverty become more strongly linked to adult poverty because being poor as a teenager has become more closely linked to being out of work as an adult, more closely linked to educational failure, or because of other more subtle linkages?

We approach the first of these questions by examining how the magnitude of the link between teenage poverty and adult poverty changes as we adjust the calculation to take account of differences between individuals in terms of their personal and family characteristics[1]. First we adjust for differences in the teenage characteristics discussed in Chapter 5, page 17. Next we adjust for differences in the adult labour market and social attributes that we found, in Chapter 5, page 21, to mediate poverty in adulthood. We then adjust for differences at both these ages to see if there is any residual impact from teenage poverty.

The essential results from this exercise are shown in Figure 3. This shows the raw odds ratios for the effect of teenage poverty on adult poverty – our main indicator of the persistence of poverty in Chapter 3 – and then shows what happens to this indicator as we allow for differences in teenage characteristics and/or adult mediators of poverty. The height of the bar (which, like all our bar-charts, is on a log-scale) indicates the strength of the direct linkage between teenage poverty and adult poverty. In some cases, our statistics tells us that we cannot be confident that there is any direct link; in these cases the bar is shown in hatched rather than solid shading.

---

[1]   We do this by including the characteristics in a logit model for adult poverty.

The first bar in each group repeats our initial finding (as shown in Figure 2), that poverty at the age of 16 has a significant link with adult poverty for teenagers in the 1970s and 1980s and that this persistence increased strongly between these two decades. The second bar in each group shows the persistence of poverty holding constant the teenage factors explored in Table 8. The *drop in height* between the first and second bars can therefore be seen as the impact of other teenage characteristics (apart from poverty) on poverty in adulthood.

Looking at this picture for teenagers in the 1970s it becomes immediately clear that *poor teenagers in the 1970s grew up to be poor because of more general family background disadvantages*, like non-employment and low education – poverty itself had little or no direct effect over and above these teenage family factors. Poor teenagers were no more likely to be poor as adults than were non-poor teenagers with otherwise similar family backgrounds. However, *for teenagers in the 1980s, poverty had a direct effect on the chances of ending up in poverty, even allowing for differences in these same aspects of family background.* Clearly some things changed between the 1970s and 1980s that made the later cohort more vulnerable in terms of transmission of poverty across generations. Certainly the poverty linkage is reduced for teenagers in the 1980s when we allow for other family background differences, but the odds of a poor teenager being a poor adult were still double those for a non-poor teenager.

In Figure 3, the third bar adjusts for differences in the adult mediators of poverty, such as education and employment, as well as the other characteristics shown in Table 9. Again, for teenagers in the 1970s, the influence of teenage poverty works through these mediators only – *poor teenagers in the 1970s were no more likely to be poor in the 1990s than their non-poor contemporaries who had similar educational and employment outcomes. But for teenage men in the 1980s the story is very different: teenage poverty links through to adult poverty even when adults have similar education, employment and other outcomes.* The picture is less clear for women, where the situation in the 1970s and 1980s seems similar. This may reflect the increasing importance of women's own characteristics in determining their poverty outcomes.

Figure 3: Association of teenage poverty with poverty in the early thirties: exploring the role of teenage disadvantage and adult mediators

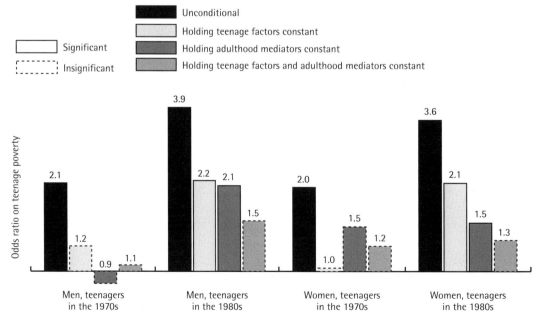

Note: Bars report odds ratios for poverty at age 16 in models of poverty at age 33/30.

Unsurprisingly perhaps, once we compare individuals with similar family background *and* similar adult mediators of poverty, being poor as a teenager has a small or very weak influence on adult poverty (the final bars in Figure 3). It is clear that in every case the characteristics we have chosen are able to almost completely explain the persistence of poverty. The task for the remainder of this report is to pinpoint these mediating factors and to understand the implications of these results for policy.

One reading of the evidence on the persistence of poverty across generations could be that there are innate, or strongly persistent, family traits – ability, motivation, psychological make-up – which mean that the parental and child outcomes are linked. This is particularly important here, because the changes in the labour market that occurred in the UK after the 1970s meant that low-ability families experienced increasingly poor outcomes – which might explain the increase in the link across generations over this period. We can explore the credibility of this hypothesis by considering the role of 'ability' in the persistence of poverty, where ability is measured by early childhood test scores[2]. Doing this actually makes little difference to the results shown in Figure 3, but this is an issue we return to later.

The specific roles of education and employment

One of the most solid results that emerged from the tables in Chapter 5 is the correlation between not working and poverty, and between low education and poverty. Employment and education seem to be the two most important channels through which poverty in childhood is fed through to adult poverty. So, we look first to these two channels for an explanation of the rise in the teenage–adult poverty linkage between the 1970s and the 1980s. The question we ask is: has the link strengthened because poor teenagers became less likely to be employed or because they became less likely to acquire a good education?

In this section we try to answer this question by considering these relationships explicitly, in a similar manner to that presented in Figure 3, but using employment in the early thirties or low education as the adult outcome. Figure 4 shows the essential results graphically. The figure shows the effect of teenage poverty on the odds of a person being in a given outcome category – non-employed, or with low educational qualifications – in their early thirties. The results are grouped by cohort and gender.

Looking at the top panel, there are some interesting findings. The 'unconditional' bars show that the raw link between poverty and employment is stronger for teenagers in the 1970s than for those in the 1980s. This change, although positive, is not significant for men, which suggests that poor teenage boys in the 1970s fared similarly to those in the 1980s in terms of subsequent employment outcomes. However, the situation changed dramatically for women: for teenage girls in the 1970s family poverty had *no* influence on adult employment outcomes, but for teenage girls in the 1980s family poverty mattered much more. This suggests that the growing association between poverty across generations may be explained by a rising link between poverty in the teenage years and unemployment/non-participation in adulthood, particularly for women. The second and third bars in each group in Figure 4(a) show what happens when we allow for differences in family background other than poverty[3]. The main finding here is that demographics and other family background attributes explain much of the link between teenage and adult poverty for boys in the 1970s. But for teenagers in the 1980s, poverty had an impact on employment above and

---

[2] The individuals in the two cohorts were both tested for reading and maths ability in childhood (at age 11 for the earlier cohort and age 10 for the later cohort).

[3] Specifically basic demographics, plus socially housed, plus sickness at age 16, plus parental employment and education.

Figure 4: Association of teenage poverty with adult non-employment and low education: exploring the role of other aspects of teenage disadvantage

(a) Non-employment as an adult outcome

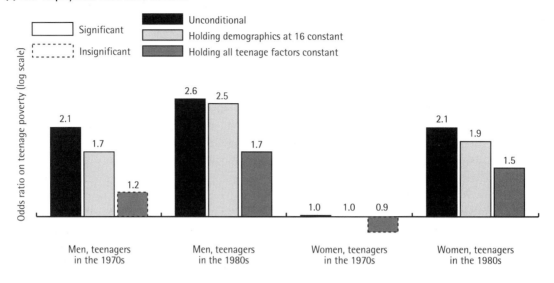

(b) Non-employment as an outcome, holding education and early measures of cognitive ability constant

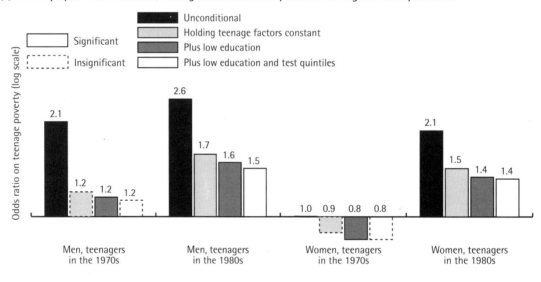

(c) Low education as an adult outcome

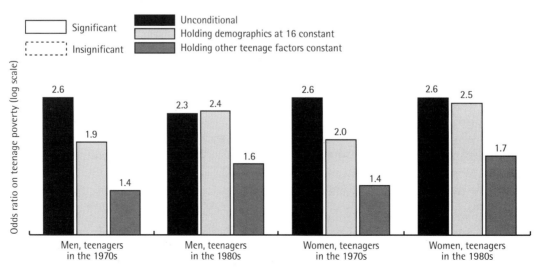

beyond what can be explained by other family background factors. Importantly too, the strength of the linkage has risen for both genders between the 1970s and the 1980s. It is notable, however, that of the teenage characteristics controlled for, mother's non-employment has a particularly strong connection with teenagers' non-employment in adulthood, and therefore drives much of the relationship between teenage poverty and adult non-employment.

While it is interesting to note the important role played by employment in determining poverty status, in order to guide policy we need to go beyond this to understand the mechanisms linking teenage poverty to employment outcomes. An obvious question to ask is whether these adverse employment outcomes could be mitigated by educational interventions. So, in the second panel of Figure 4(b) we explore the role of educational attainment and cognitive ability (proxied by the scores from maths and reading tests described above). The first and second bars present the unconditional effects and the effects conditional on family background that we saw in Figure 4(a). Next, the third bar takes account of low educational attainment in adulthood alongside these teenage factors, while the fourth bar compares outcomes for teenagers with similar levels of childhood cognitive ability. For all cohort and gender groups, allowing for these differences in education and/or cognitive ability makes little difference to our finding that the influence of teenage poverty on adult poverty increased between the 1970s and 1980s.

A more direct approach to evaluating the role of educational attainments is taken in Figure 4(c). This uses the same techniques, but models low education (less than O level) as an individual outcome. Teenage poverty is always associated with low educational attainments, even when comparing teenagers with similar family background characteristics[4]. However, in contrast to the non-employment results, the simple association between teenage poverty and low educational attainments fell slightly for boys, and only rose slightly for girls between the 1970s and 1980s. Once we take account of family demographics, there is stronger evidence of an upward shift in the link from teenage poverty to low educational attainments over the decade[5]. However, the shift is small when compared with the overall change between the cohorts that we see in Figure 3. Taken together with the results in Figure 4(b) it appears that changing relationships between cognitive ability, education and poverty are not able to explain the rise in the persistence of poverty.

The examination of the relationship between education and employment and teenage poverty has mixed success in helping us to understand why teenagers in the 1980s were more strongly affected by poverty in the family than teenagers in the 1970s. There does seem to be some evidence that poverty at the age of 16 has become more strongly associated with adult employment outcomes, which may help to explain the rising link between poverty across generations. The results for education do not show this pattern.

---

[4] Blanden et al (2004) stressed how a growing association between educational attainment and parental income was able to partly explain the rise in persistence between parental income and earnings. However, this association is strongly driven by the association between higher education attainment, rather than low education. This relationship is discussed in detail in Blanden and Machin (2004).

[5] In particular, the number of children in the household appears to be driving the correlation between poverty at 16 and low education among teens in the 1970s. Poorer families have more children and growing up in a larger family negatively impacts on educational attainment (see Black et al, 2004, for a recent consideration of family size and birth order effects on educational attainment). This prediction is fairly standard in economics (see Becker and Lewis, 1973) and it is interesting that it is found among the first cohort, but not for the second.

The role of other factors that are related to adverse employment outcomes

As childhood factors seem unable to explain the rise in persistence, we now shift the focus of the discussion to the role of other characteristics in the early thirties. By discovering the adult characteristics associated with non-employment we may find additional clues as to the routes through which poverty in the teenage years is associated with later non-employment. Table 11 shows the conditional odds ratios between non-employment in the early thirties and other characteristics at this age. For men in the 1990s and both genders in 2000 these factors account for 18%-19% of the variance in employment outcomes. The characteristics play less of a role for women in the 1990s, explaining only around 8% of the variance.

Two of the most important relationships that appear here are between employment and having a limiting health condition (for both sexes) and between employment and lone parenthood for women. It is possible that further investigation of these mechanisms could help uncover more about the relationship between poverty at different ages.

Taking health problems first, earlier analysis of disadvantage showed that health problems and poverty are related in the early thirties, although this link is explained entirely because those with limiting health difficulties are less likely to work. Health problems are therefore a potential mediator between poverty at different ages: those who experience childhood poverty are more likely to develop health difficulties, and these lead to non-employment and poverty.

In Figure 5(a) we explore the connection between a limiting health problem and teenage poverty, holding teenage factors constant as before. It is immediately striking that teenage girls who were poor in the 1980s grew up to have much higher odds of having a limiting health condition than did their 1970s counterparts. Moreover, teenage poverty has a direct link with adult ill health over and above all the other age 16 characteristics. For men, there is little change, although the relationship for teenagers in the 1980s is much more statistically robust than for the earlier cohort. While the rising importance of poverty in determining health difficulties is interesting in itself, it is more difficult to relate this story to the changes in persistence we have found. As shown in earlier results, the link between

Table 11: Mediators of individual non-employment in adulthood

| | Conditional odds ratios | | | |
	Men aged 33 in 1991	Men aged 30 in 2000	Women aged 33 in 1991	Women aged 30 in 2000
Single	2.90	1.38	0.75	1.03
Number of children in household	1.20	1.32	1.55	2.30
Lone parent	1.91	0.98	2.26	1.71
Non-white	1.17	1.45	0.75	1.00
Council tenant	4.53	4.50	1.83	1.86
Limiting health condition	5.48	4.80	1.98	2.75
Low education cohort member	2.13	1.72	1.46	1.43
Low education partner	1.30	0.92	0.67	0.74

Notes: Conditional odds ratios report the odds ratio between non-employment at age 33/30 and the characteristic in a multivariate model with all the other characteristics also included.

Bold: less than 5% chance of no real difference between the groups in the population.

Sample sizes: 1991: men 4,026, women 5,747; 2000: men 5,347, women 5,673.

limiting health problems, unemployment and poverty are most important for men, yet the strongest rise in the correlation between poverty and health problems is found for women.

A similar argument can be explored for girls growing up to become lone parents. If teenage poverty raises the chances of childbirth outside of a relationship or later family break up, this could be a route generating the persistence of disadvantage across generations[6]. Figure 5(b) presents our findings on the link between women's lone parenthood and their earlier poverty. Once again, teenage poverty has a larger impact on the outcome in the second cohort; the odds ratio is 1.7 for women who were teenagers in the 1970s and 2.4 for

Figure 5: Association of teenage poverty with other adult mediators of poverty: the role of other aspects of teenage disadvantage

(a) Limiting illness in the thirties

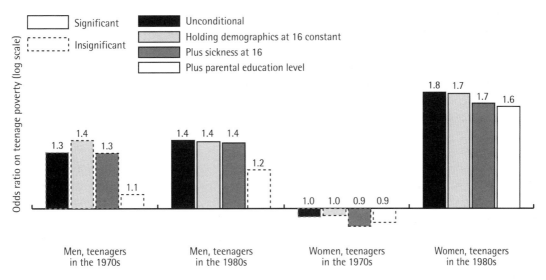

(b) Lone parent in the thirties (women only)

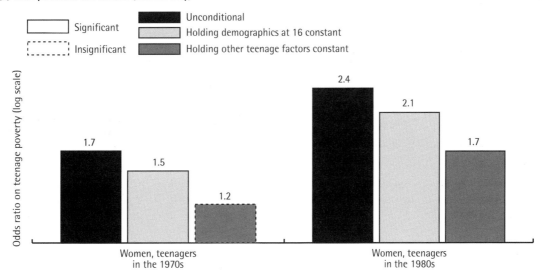

Note: Bars report odds ratios for poverty at age 16 in models of being (a) limiting health condition; (b) female lone parent at age 33/30.

---

6   It is possible that the causality between poverty and family breakdown may go the other way, so that tensions introduced by financial difficulty lead to relationship break up. To make some sense of the mechanisms, it is necessary to make some assumptions on the direction of causation.

those who were teenagers in the 1980s. This provides a possible explanation for the rising relationship between poverty across generations for women: teenagers in the 1980s were much more likely to grow up to become lone parents than they were in the 1970s.

One potential mediator between teenage poverty and lone parenthood in adulthood, might be the teenager's own experience of growing up in a lone-mother family. Results from Hobcraft and Kiernan (1997) and Kiernan and Cherlin (1999) suggest that parental divorce in childhood is likely to lead to a higher probability of lone parenthood for adults both through pre-marital conception and partnership dissolution. We have seen that living with a lone mother was linked with poverty as a teenager, and this coupled with a link in lone-mother status could explain the persistence of poverty shown in the first bar. The second bar in Figure 5(b) shows the effect of teenage poverty when we compare those with similar teenage family characteristics (lone mother, number of other children in the household, non-white ethnicity). If it were the case that the relationship with poverty worked through links in lone-parent status across generations (and a link between teenage poverty and being in a lone-mother family), then the impact of poverty at 16 would be wiped out by controlling for these variables. There does seem to be some effect of demographic persistence, as the odds ratio on poverty falls between the first and second bars. However, the link between teenage poverty and adult lone parenthood remains strong, and for the second cohort there is a relationship between teenage poverty and later lone parenthood even taking into account differences in all other aspects of family background disadvantage. These results suggest that for teenagers in the 1980s there was a link between poverty and later lone motherhood that is independent of their teenage family characteristics. This link could come about either because women who were poor teenagers had characteristics that made their relationships more likely to break down and/or their poor upbringings led them to be more likely to have children outside of relationships. If the second, then it appears that recent government interventions to discourage teenage childbearing may be well placed to reduce the persistence of poverty for women.

Key points

In the 1970s, the reasons that poverty for teenagers linked through to poverty in later life were almost all attributable to other attributes of the family in which they lived – particularly lack of employment and low education. By the 1980s, being poor as a teenager seems to have played an increasingly independent role in engendering poverty in later life. This is because teenage poverty became more closely linked to the likelihood of a person being out of work in their early thirties. The main factors linked to being out of work in adulthood are low education, lone parenthood and ill health. However, educational attainment does not explain the rise in persistence: the risk of poor teenagers in the 1980s ending up without qualifications was not much greater than for poor teenagers in the 1970s. Compared with a girl in the 1970s, a poor teenage girl in the 1980s was at higher risk for lone parenthood and at higher risk for incapacity through illness in her thirties. These facts can explain part, although not all, of the rise in the intergenerational persistence over this period – but only for women.

7

Explaining the persistence of poverty through to middle age

Our earlier results (Table 6) demonstrated that the link between teenage poverty and adult poverty extended through to middle age, with the size of the transmission similar at ages 33 and 42. While some of the association between teenage and middle age poverty can be explained by links through poverty in a person's thirties, there is also a direct link between teenage and middle aged poverty. To understand more about the factors behind these links we once again use 'conditional' models to try and evaluate the extent to which the links between poverty at different ages are transmitted through mediating factors, both in the teenage years and when the cohort members are adults. Figure 6 shows what happens to the size of the link between the teenage poverty, early adulthood poverty (42) and middle age poverty (42) as we change the factors that are held constant when making comparisons between individuals.

The first bars in the figures repeat the results from column 2 of Table 6. They show that while there is a very strong relationship between poverty in the early thirties and poverty in middle age, teenage poverty also has a direct impact on the chances of being poor in middle age. However, the second pair of bars shows the odds ratios when we compare people who had similar teenage family background in other ways apart from family poverty. When we do this, the direct effect of teenage poverty becomes small and statistically weak showing that the persistence of direct effects from teenage poverty through to middle age can be fully explained by the other aspects of teenage disadvantage. This means that whether or not you are poor in middle age really depends on whether you had low-educated or non-employed parents, rather than whether you were poor as a teenager. We can go further, and take account of the mediators of poverty in the early thirties and in middle age. The results for this exercise are shown in the remaining bars of Figure 6. Interpreting these results, it seems that teenage family background feeds through to middle age poverty over and above poverty in the thirties to a slightly greater extent for women than for men. However, for the most part, teenage poverty makes little difference to the chances of middle age poverty once we compare individuals with similar poverty outcomes in their thirties, similar adult characteristics and similar family background.

Figure 6: Association of teenage and adult poverty with middle age poverty

(a) Men

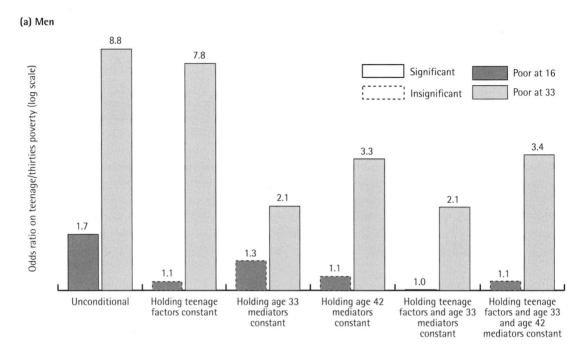

(b) Women

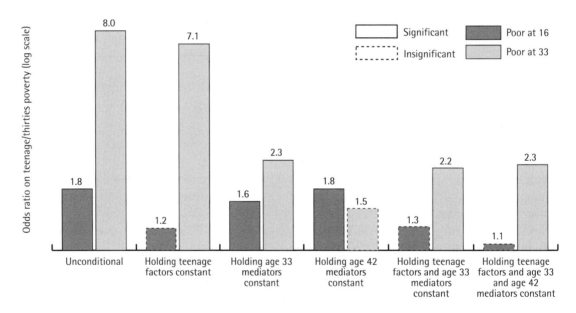

Note: Bars report odds ratios for the effect of poverty at ages 16 and 33 on age 42 poverty

8

Summary

If the experience of poverty in childhood leads to poverty in later life, then children brought up in poverty are disadvantaged not just by their immediate circumstances but by persistent effects throughout their lifecycle. This in turn can lead to disadvantages for their children and future generations of the same dynasty. Clearly then, an understanding of whether poverty persists in this way is vital for informing policy aimed at tackling childhood disadvantage. This report is motivated by the need to understand this process in the UK. The principal goals have been to measure the extent to which poverty persists over different stages of the lifecycle and to find out if this has changed over recent decades. In addition, the aim has been to shed some light on why this transmission occurs.

The main questions this report has asked are:

1. Is poverty in a person's childhood associated with poverty in their adulthood and middle age?
2. If there is a link, has it become stronger or weaker over recent decades?
3. Is the link between teenage poverty and adult poverty really a result of poverty, or is adult poverty more closely linked to other family background characteristics?
4. What factors can explain changes in the persistence of poverty over time?

The short answers to these questions are:

1. Children who are poor as teenagers are more likely than those who are not poor to grow up to be poor adults. This is true through to middle age.
2. Comparing two of the most recent cohorts we can observe into adulthood – teenagers in the 1970s and teenagers in the 1980s – we find a large increase in the association of teenage poverty and subsequent adult poverty.
3. In the 1970s, the fact that poor teenagers became poor adults was attributable to basic family background factors like low-educated and workless parents. By the 1980s, poverty seems to have come to play a more direct role. Poor teenagers in the 1980s were at a higher risk of adult poverty than non-poor teenagers from similar family backgrounds.
4. The increase in the persistence of poverty over the decades is a result of the fact that teenage poverty became more closely linked to adult worklessness. It is harder to pin down why this change happened. Changes in educational attainment are not to blame, but higher risk of poor health and lone parenthood are possible explanations.

So, we have two important new findings on the extent of the persistence of poverty. The first is that the persistence of poverty from the teens into the early thirties has risen over time, with teenage poverty having a greater impact on later outcomes for teenagers in the 1980s compared with teenagers in the 1970s. This is in line with the results in Blanden et al (2004) showing an increase in the influence of family income at age 16 on earnings in the early thirties. This report has therefore added to the wider evidence that family background has had a growing impact on later outcomes between these cohorts.

The second major finding shows that the link between poverty in teens and adulthood continues to have a bearing through to middle age for the cohort who were teenagers in the 1970s (born in 1958). This is the case regardless of whether or not the person was poor in their thirties. In other words, an adult who was a poor teenager continues to be at higher risk of poverty by middle age even if they managed to get out of poverty in their thirties. Moreover, the links between poverty in a person's early thirties and early forties are very strong, so there is a knock-on effect to middle age for those driven into poverty in early adulthood because of childhood experiences. It is also clear that the persistence of poverty between ages within adulthood is much more important than any transmissions between parents and children. An implication that could be drawn from this is that addressing the adulthood causes of poverty directly is likely to be much more beneficial over adults' lifecycles than tackling poverty faced in childhood. However, the strong link between adult and middle age poverty is likely to be indicative of the strength of the persistence of poverty-causing characteristics in adults, something that would be hard to address with later interventions. There may be lower costs of effective intervention at an early stage, when these poverty-related attributes are not fully developed.

In part, the motivation behind this report is prompted by the government's stated policy to reduce child poverty and ameliorate its consequences. It is therefore natural to look for policy recommendations in our results. However, it is important to remember that the two cohorts considered in this report were born in 1958 and 1970 and therefore grew up in completely different environments throughout their lifecycle than those who are children now in the 2000s. Nevertheless, our primary findings – that poverty in childhood has long-term consequences and that the importance of these long-term consequences grew for the second cohort relative to the first – lead us to believe that children growing up in poverty now may face similar disadvantages to these earlier cohorts. On this basis, isolation of specific channels through which poverty persisted across generations in the past would be relevant for policy aimed at tackling childhood poverty now. Indeed, those who we observe in poverty in their teenage years may now be parents themselves, possibly leading to another generation being affected by the initial disadvantage.

A central question in this respect is whether it is lack of money in itself that leads to poorer outcomes in adulthood, or whether poverty is simply a summary measure of the numerous facets of disadvantage faced by poor teenagers, such as poor parental education, lack of employment in the family and family type. If low income itself has implications for children's lifecycle outcomes then the appropriate intervention is to redistribute income to ensure that children are lifted out of poverty. Our results suggest, on balance, that income itself is not the main cause and that broader teenage disadvantage is the major driver of the persistence of poverty across the generations in both cohorts. On this basis – since many of these background disadvantages cannot be changed for parents of the current generation of children – the policy recommendation must be to intervene to address the consequences of these disadvantages and to weaken their development in subsequent generations.

However, although the increase in the link between poverty across generations can be explained in part by a stronger impact of measured disadvantage, we must emphasise that there is a strong impact of poverty over and above other measured disadvantages in the 1980s, which was not experienced by those growing up in the 1970s. This provides some grounds for suggesting that redistribution could have had a beneficial impact for those growing up in the later cohort, but it is of course difficult to know whether this still applies to the generation of children growing up now.

Since our results indicate only a limited role for redistribution, we must consider whether other policies could break the link between disadvantage and poor outcomes for children. Yet when we consider the range of possible factors that contribute to childhood disadvantage and poverty it is difficult to single out any as the most appropriate target for interventions. It is not possible to explain the strength of transmission or its increase between the 1970s and 1980s entirely by one (or even two) factors. If all the relationship between poverty across generations were explicable by poor children doing less well at school, or by poor health, or by early motherhood, then these would be obvious policy targets. But our results indicate that this is not the case. Although lack of education is an important cause of adverse adult outcomes, it cannot explain the *rising* link between poverty across generations. Certainly poor children are less likely to be employed in later life and this is the main contributory factor to adult poverty, but there is no single factor that explains why poor children suffer in this way or why the problem increased between the 1970s and 1980s. Among the many other factors in family background we have considered here, most matter to some degree and it would be misleading to highlight any one as dominant. These findings suggest that initiatives to improve skills and employment opportunities are probably the only sensible way to tackle the problem of persistent poverty and that there is no quick fix available through other more specific interventions. This finding is not because of inadequate methods or poor data; it is because the causes are multidimensional. Despite the lack of specific policy prescriptions that can be drawn out of our work, it is completely clear that children in poverty are more likely to grow up to be poor, and that, as far as we can tell, this link has strengthened over the last decades of the 20th century.

References

Atkinson, A.B. (1987) 'On the Measurement of Poverty', *Econometrica*, vol 55, pp 479-764.

Becker, G. and Lewis, H.G. (1973) 'On the Interaction between the Quantity and Quality of Children', *Journal of Political Economy*, vol 81, pp S279-S288.

Black, S., Devereux, P. and Salvanes, K. (2004) *The More the Merrier? The Effect of Family Composition on Children's Education*, NBER Working Paper No 10720 (www.nber.org).

Blanden, J. and Machin, S. (2004) 'Educational Inequality and the Expansion of UK Higher Education', *Scottish Journal of Political Economy*, vol 51, pp 230-49.

Blanden, J., Goodman, A., Gregg, P. and Machin, S. (2004) 'Changes in Intergenerational Mobility in Britain', in M. Corak (ed) *Generational Income Mobility in North America and Europe*, Cambridge: Cambridge University Press.

Brewer, M., Clark, T., Goodman, A., Shaw, J. and Shephard, A. (2005) *Poverty and Inequality in Britain 2005*, Commentary No 99, London: Institute for Fiscal Studies.

Bynner, J., Elias, P., McKnight, A., Pan, H. and Pierre, G. (2002) *Young People's Changing Route to Independence*, York: Joseph Rowntree Foundation.

Freeman, R. (1984) 'Longitudinal Analysis of Trade Unions', *Journal of Labor Economics*, vol 2, pp 1-26.

Grawe, N. (2004) 'The 3-day Week of 1974 and Earnings Data Reliability in the Family Expenditure Survey and the National Child Development Survey', *Oxford Bulletin of Economics and Statistics*, vol 66, pp 567-79.

Gregg, P. and Machin, S. (1999) 'Childhood Disadvantage and Success or Failure in the Labour Market', in D. Blanchflower and R. Freeman (eds) *Youth Employment and Joblessness in Advanced Countries*, Cambridge, MA: National Bureau of Economic Research.

Gregg, P., Hansen, K. and Wadsworth, J. (1999a) 'The Rise of the Workless Household', in *The State of Working Britain*, Manchester: Manchester University Press.

Gregg, P., Harkness, S. and Machin, S. (1999b) 'Poor Kids: Trends in Child Poverty in Britain, 1968-1996', *Fiscal Studies*, vol 20, pp 163-87.

Heath, A. (1981) *Social Mobility*, London: Fontana.

Hobcraft. J.N. (2003) *Continuity and Change in Pathways to Young Adult Disadvantage: Results from a British Birth Cohort*, CASEpaper 66, London: Centre for Analysis of Social Exclusion, London School of Economics and Political Science.

Hobcraft, J.N. (2004) 'Parental, Childhood and Early Adult Legacies in the Emergence of Adult Social Exclusion: Evidence on What Matters from a British Cohort', in P.L Chase-Lansdale, K.E. Kiernan and R.J. Friedman (eds) *Human Development Across Lives and Generations: The Potential for Change, Cambridge:* Cambridge University Press.

Hobcraft, J.N. and Kiernan, K. (1997) 'Parental Divorce during Childhood: Age at First Intercourse, Partnership and Parenthood', *Population Studies*, vol 51, pp 41-55.

Jarvis, S. and Jenkins, S. (1997) 'Low Income Dynamics in 1990s Britain', *Fiscal Studies*, vol 8, pp 123-42.

Kiernan, K. and Cherlin, A. (1999) 'Parental Divorce and Partnership Dissolution in Adulthood: Evidence from a British Cohort Study', *Population Studies*, vol 53, pp 39-48.

McClements, L. (1977) 'Equivalence Scales for Children', *Journal of Public Economics*, vol 8, pp 191-210.

Micklewright, J. (1986) *A Note on Household Income Data in NCDS 3*, National Child Development Study User Group, London: City University.

National Sure Start Evaluation (2004) 'The Impact of Sure Start Local Programmes on Child Development and Family Functioning: A Report on Preliminary Findings' (available at www.ness.bbk.ac.uk/documents/activities/impact/397.pdf).

ONS (Office for National Statistics) (2004) *Birth Statistics: Review of the Registrar General on Births and Patterns of Family Building in England and Wales, 2003*, London: ONS (www.statistics.gov.uk/downloads/theme_population/FM1_32/FM1no32.pdf).

Appendix: Data quality and robustness checks

In order to be confident about the analysis presented in the main part of this report, we need to demonstrate that the income data on which much of the analysis is based is not leading to any biases. There are three dimensions of this that are explored in this Appendix. First, the way the income data from the cohorts is generated is discussed, then this data is compared with income data from the Family Expenditure Survey (FES) for similar families, to check if the distributions of income observed appear sensible compared with data from a survey which is more explicitly designed to gather information about income. These comparisons were discussed to a certain extent in Chapter 2. The second, and more substantive, dimension of this Appendix is to consider the implications of attrition and non-response in the datasets used and to highlight the ways in which these limitations of the data will influence the results.

The parental income data used to define poverty at the age of 16 is not provided in an ideal form in either cohort. The information on the National Child Development Study (NCDS) income is presented by source 'father's earnings', 'mother's earnings' and 'other income'. In each case parents are asked to provide information by selecting the band into which their net weekly or monthly income from each source falls. There is some ambiguity in terms of what missing reports for each component mean: does it mean that families have no income from this source or simply that the information is missing? If it is the case that a component is missing then there is an argument for dropping the observation. This issue is considered in some detail in a data note by Micklewright (1986), and we have followed his advice in excluding families where a parent's earnings are missing but they are reported to be working in another part of the questionnaire. The British Cohort Study (BCS) parental income data is not reported by component. Instead, parents are asked to indicate which band (from 11) their gross total weekly income falls into.

In order to use banded data as an explanatory variable in the usual intergenerational model we must convert it into a continuous form. For the NCDS we assign each component a single value which is the midpoint for this component for similar families in this band in the FES in 1974. Family income is generated by summing these variables. Combining information on three components means that the final income distribution has 77 different values. For the BCS, where there is only one banded variable, we use maximum likelihood estimation to model a Singh-Maddala distribution for the data. In principle, it should also be possible to estimate the distribution based on the 77 unique categories in the NCDS, but the fact that the upper and lower bounds for the categories are not exclusive means that this is computationally impractical.

The methods of data collection indicate some clear problems with the comparability of the parental income data across the cohorts. First, there are clearly many more unique values possible for the NCDS than the BCS. Second, the NCDS income components are reported as net of tax while the BCS asks for gross income. To account for this, we refer across to the FES data for the appropriate year (in this case 1986) where incomes are reported both net and gross. We can then calculate the proportion paid in tax by families in each band. We subtract the median of this from the expected value obtained in the Singh-Maddala distribution[1]. The final difficulty is that the NCDS income question clearly asks parents to

---

[1] The proportion subtracted in tax is 0 for the first two income bands (up to £100 a week in 1986 prices) and rises up to 26% in the top income band (those with incomes of £500 or more).

include Child Benefit, whereas the BCS data asks that it be excluded. We therefore impute a value for Child Benefit based on the number of children in the household (and lone-parent status for the BCS as this was relevant to Child Benefit entitlements in 1986).

There is one final concern with the parental income data, which relates to the NCDS only. In 1974, when the age 16 data was being collected for this cohort, the UK was in the midst of a three-day working week due to a power shortage brought about by unrest in the coal industry. The worry is that parents would report their incomes from a three-day week rather than their usual incomes. Grawe (2004) considers this difficulty by comparing reported father's earnings across the period when the three-day week was in effect with information gathered after it had ended. The study seems to find convincingly that few income reports have additional measurement error due to the exceptional circumstances and Grawe states that his best estimate of the fraction of misreports is 0.

Compared with these difficulties, using the income data reported by adult cohort members is relatively straightforward. The cohort member is asked to report recent income receipts by component and give the length of time that the payment covers. Some fairly substantial cleaning of these data was required as often the amount and pay period did not match up: the Institute for Fiscal Studies' tax and benefit information was very useful in carrying out this cleaning.

Figures A1-A5 and Tables A1 and A2 draw comparisons between the income data in the cohorts and income recorded in the FES for samples of similar households (which include individuals of similar ages). As discussed in Chapter 2, one of the main problems revealed is the higher number of households below the poverty line in the age 16 data for the cohort studies. Apart from this feature, income data appears to match up fairly well. It is hoped that by experimenting with alternative measures of poverty, the results shown in the main section have been revealed to be relatively robust to difficulties in using the cohort data to define poverty.

Table A1: Quality of the childhood income data

Group	NCDS 16 Cohort members	FES 1974 Age 10-16	BCS 10 Cohort members	FES 1980 Age 7-13	BCS 16 Cohort members	FES 1986 Age 10-16
Mean income	46.39 [8,856]	56.72 [1,361]	114.10 [11,451]	134.44 [1,484]	190.55 [7,152]	220.05 [1,255]
Median income	47.45	51.93	107.16	125.48	165.91	195.85
Mean equivalised income	29.51 [8,856]	36.99 [1,360]	73.35 [11,449]	89.92 [1,484]	123.16 [7,128]	151.81 [1,255]
Median equivalised income	30.70	33.41	70.50	83.36	108.54	133.32
60% median poverty line from FES population	28.89	20.80	51.82	51.82	83.09	83.09
Poverty rate using FES line	0.223	0.138	0.192	0.133	0.267	0.155
Poverty rate – full population		0.144 [6,541]		0.127 [6,801]		0.124 [7,038]

Table A2: Quality of the adult income data

Group	NCDS 33 Cohort members	FES 1991 Age 30–36	NCDS 42 Cohort members	FES 2000 Age 39–45	BCS 30 Cohort members	FES 2000 Age 27–33
Some earnings	0.889 [7,755]	0.851 [1,131]	0.902 [8,183]	0.845 [1,026]	0.900 [9,144]	0.828 [1,159]
Mean head and partner's earnings	298.26 [6,896]	287.24 [1,010]	490.61 [7,382]	421.63 [913]	419.06 [8,234]	410.01 [997]
Median head and partner's earnings	272.43	272.27	420.93	393.93	370	364.51
Mean head and partner's benefit	34.64 [5,483]	63.60 [818]	62.95 [5,934]	89.10 [864]	73.87 [4,551]	90.09 [861]
Median head and partner's benefit	15.50	33.50	34	48	34	48
Mean income	294.72 [7,765]	310.12 [1,131]	503.48 [8,183]	457.15 [1,026]	422.36 [9,144]	423.85 [1,159]
Median income	272.48	286.19	435.16	411.41	372.84	367.85
Mean equivalised income	278.44 [7,748]	301.25 [1,129]	422.33 [8,155]	413.55 [1,026]	457.53 [9,027]	437.44 [1,159]
Median equivalised income	239.68	247.8	351.62	365.14	399	377.59
60% median poverty line from FES population	131.12	131.12	192.35	192.35	192.35	192.35
Poverty rate using FES line	0.160	0.136	0.134	0.135	0.107	0.154
Poverty rate – full population		0.196 [6,211]		0.170 [5,943]		0.170 [5,943]

Figure A1: NCDS equivalent income at age 16, compared with the FES

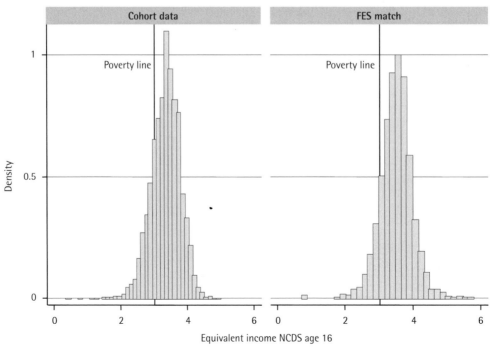

Source: Graphs by FES.

Figure A2: BCS equivalent income at age 16, compared with the FES

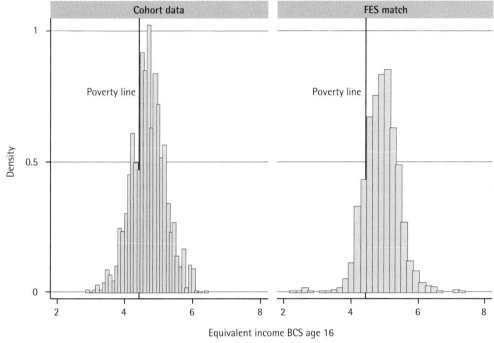

Source: Graphs by FES.

Figure A3: NCDS equivalent income at age 33, compared with the FES

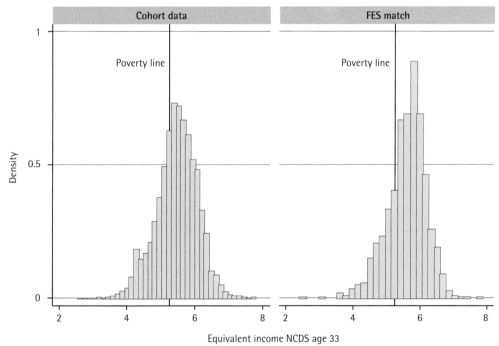

Source: Graphs by FES.

Figure A4: BCS equivalent income at age 30, compared with the FES

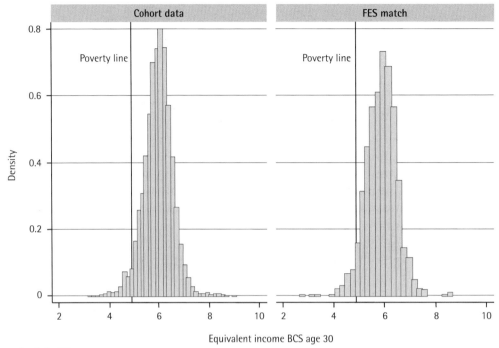

Source: Graphs by FES.

Figure A5: NCDS equivalent income at age 42, compared with the FES

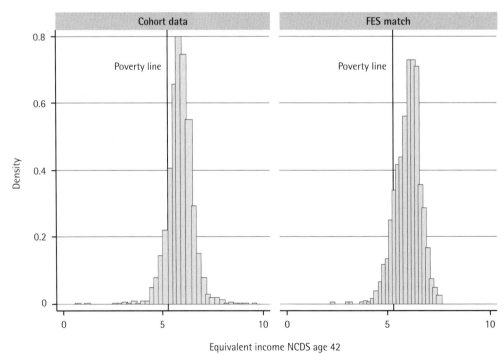

Source: Graphs by FES.

In the main analysis around 5,000 observations are used for each cohort to measure the persistence of poverty between age 16 and age 33/30; this is approximately one quarter of the total number of individuals who started life in each cohort. This large reduction in the sample is a consequence of individuals being lost from the sample as they age (attrition) and individuals' refusal to answer key components of the survey (most importantly, for our purposes, the income questions). These cumulative losses will not matter greatly for the results if the smaller sample that remains is representative of the original cohort. What is more of a problem is if the nature of the sample becomes more or less advantaged because of the sample losses. In particular we will be particularly concerned about the finding that the persistence of poverty has changed across cohorts if the non-response and attrition has changed systematically between the cohorts.

Tables A3, A4 and A5 document the causes of the small samples in the cohorts, showing where observations are lost due to attrition and non-response, and demonstrating how the samples fall to one quarter of their original size.

While the sample reductions are worrying in themselves (as they will reduce the precision of our estimates), what is of most concern is how the sample reductions impact on the representativeness of the final samples. In order to explore this, we show how the means and standard deviations of particular characteristics change for the reduced samples compared with those we started with. In order to do this, it is necessary to consider variables with a high response rate. We consider social class (obtained at age 7 for the NCDS and age 5 for the BCS) and reading and maths scores at age 11/10, as well as later measures of poverty and education.

In terms of the overall sample selections, there is evidence that the final samples for both cohorts have higher parental status and child outcomes than if non-response and attrition did not affect the surveys. Unfortunately, there is also some evidence that this problem is more acute in the BCS than the NCDS. To illustrate: the average social class index of the NCDS is 3.76 for all male cohort members compared with 3.73 for the persistence of poverty sample; in the BCS the difference is 3.55 compared with 3.40.

Table A3: Attrition in the cohort studies

	NCDS	
	Men	Women
All cohort members	9,593	8,960
In at age 7	0.825	0.836
In at age 11	0.821	0.831
In at age 16	0.787	0.793
In at age 23	0.653	0.700
In at age 33	0.584	0.647
In at age 42	0.587	0.646
	BCS	
	Men	Women
All cohort members	9,643	8,903
In at age 5	0.704	0.708
In at age 10	0.800	0.805
In at age 16	0.603	0.651
In at age 30	0.560	0.645

Table A4: Item non-response in the cohort studies

	NCS Proportion in the relevant sweep with a valid observation	
	Men	Women
Income at 16	0.607	0.608
Staying on at 23	0.996	0.998
Education information at 23	0.999	1
Employment status at 33	0.996	0.997
Usable income at 33	0.700	0.667
Usable income at 42	0.721	0.719

	BCS Proportion in the relevant sweep with a valid observation	
	Men	Women
Income at 10	0.840	0.847
Income at 16	0.613	0.624
Education information at 30	0.994	0.996
Employment status at 30	0.991	0.992
Usable income at 30	0.813	0.820

Table A5: The combined effect of attrition and non-response

	NCDS Proportion of all cohort members	
Variables	Men	Women
Income at 16	0.478	0.482
Income at 16 and education at 23	0.378	0.402
Income at 16 and income at 33	0.238	0.252
Income at 16, income at 33 and 42	0.173	0.187

	BCS Proportion of all cohort members	
Variables	Men	Women
Income at 10	0.671	0.681
Income at 16	0.370	0.406
Income at 10 and 16	0.313	0.347
Income at 16 and education at 30	0.271	0.330
Income at 16 and income at 30	0.225	0.274
Income at 10 and 16 and income at 30	0.194	0.234

Table A6: The impact of attrition and non-response on sample characteristics – NCDS

	Father's social class (age 7)	Reading percentile (age 11)	Maths percentile (age 11)	Poor at 16	Education category (age 33)	Poor at 33	Poor at 42
Men							
All cohort members	3.76 (1.25) [7,228]	48.10 (29.58) [7,257]	49.53 (29.62) [7,255]	0.225 (0.418) [4,584]	4.18 (2.62) [7,137]	0.124 (0.329) [3,920]	0.118 (0.322) [4,041]
Income at 16	3.81 (1.21) [3,904]	48.97 (29.52) [3,988]	50.66 (29.44) [3,987]	0.225 (0.417) [4,584]	4.26 (2.58) [4,030]	0.120 (0.325) [2,281]	0.115 (0.319) [2,367]
Income at 16 and education at 23	3.78 (1.21) [3,139]	50.29 (29.42) [3,204]	52.09 (29.06) [3,203]	0.206 (0.405) [3,633]	4.28 (2.57) [3,633]	0.109 (0.312) [1,991]	0.109 (0.311) [2,029]
Income at 16 and income at 33	3.77 (1.21) [2,000]	51.95 (29.03) [2,001]	53.89 (29.02) [2,001]	0.213 (0.409) [2,282]	4.63 (2.50) [2,280]	0.120 (0.324) [2,281]	0.097 (0.296) [1,652]
Income at 16, income at 33 and income at 42	3.76 (1.20) [1,453]	52.60 (28.8) [1,470]	55.07 (28.66) [1,470]	0.200 (0.400) [1,657]	4.78 (2.46) [1,655]	0.097 (0.296) [1,656]	0.097 (0.296) [1,655]
Women							
All cohort members	3.76 (1.24) [6,888]	48.41 (29.21) [6,876]	49.69 (28.45) [6,874]	0.223 (0.417) [4,317]	4.01 (2.63) [7,027]	0.193 (0.395) [3,866]	0.152 (0.359) [4,153]
Income at 16	3.81 (1.21) [3,715]	48.93 (28.51) [3,778]	48.79 (28.35) [3,776]	0.223 (0.417) [4,317]	4.06 (2.58) [3,949]	0.198 (0.398) [2,256]	0.150 (0.357) [2,392]
Income at 16 and education at 30	3.79 (1.22) [3,144]	49.74 (27.92) [3,196]	50.88 (28.14) [3,195]	0.215 (0.411) [3,600]	4.08 (2.57) [3,600]	0.190 (0.392) [2,024]	0.141 (0.349) [2,128]
Income at 16 and income at 33	3.82 (1.22) [1,957]	49.75 (27.66) [1,994]	50.77 (28.06) [1,994]	0.225 (0.418) [2,257]	4.22 (2.56) [2,257]	0.198 (0.398) [2,256]	0.147 (0.354) [1,676]
Income at 16, income at 33 and income at 42	3.80 (1.22) [1,466]	50.19 (27.45) [1,488]	52.11 (27.61) [1,488]	0.221 (0.415) [1,677]	4.27 (2.53) [1,677]	0.187 (0.390) [1,677]	0.147 (0.354) [1,676]

Notes: See Table A7(a)

Table A7(a): The impact of attrition and non-response on sample characteristics – BCS men

	Father's social class (age 5)	Reading percentile (age 10)	Maths percentile (age 10)	Poor at 16	Education category (age 30)	Poor at 30
All cohort members	3.54 (1.27) [6,349]	47.59 (28.96) [6,604]	50.60 (29.67) [6,028]	0.268 (0.443) [3,555]	4.69 (2.60) [5362]	0.094 (0.292) [4324]
Income at 10	3.55 (1.26) [5,080]	48.21 (28.89) [5,512]	51.23 (29.58) [5,092]	0.258 (0.439) [3,003]	4.69 (2.59) [4326]	0.091 (0.287) [3524]
Income at 16	3.51 (1.26) [2,836]	50.73 (28.99) [2,968]	53.65 (29.70) [2,732]	0.268 (0.443) [3,555]	4.90 (2.55) [2605]	0.078 (0.268) [2144]
Income at 10 and 16	3.51 (1.27) [2,484]	51.07 (28.80) [2,638]	53.95 (29.64) [2,444]	0.258 (0.437) [3,003]	4.92 (2.54) [2249]	0.078 (0.268) [1871]
Income at 16 and education	3.46 (1.27) [2,133]	52.29 (28.72) [2,223]	55.17 (29.31) [2,059]	0.245 (0.430) [2,602]	4.90 (2.55) [2604]	0.078 (0.269) [2143]
Income at 16 and income at 30	3.45 (1.27) [1,768]	52.50 (28.72) [1,868]	55.31 (29.39) [1,722]	0.249 (0.432) [2,168]	4.96 (2.55) [2168]	0.078 (0.268) [2144]
Income at 10, income at 16 and income at 30	3.45 (1.27) [1,563]	52.69 (28.70) [1,677]	55.58 (29.41) [1,548]	0.242 (0.429) [1,868]	4.98 (2.54) [1867]	0.078 (0.269) [1851]

Notes:

1. Standard deviations are in parentheses.
2. Sample sizes are in square brackets.
3. The father's social class variable has six categories: (1) Professional ; (2) Intermediate; (3) Skilled non-manual ; (4) Skilled manual ; (5) Semi-skilled; (6) Unskilled. A fall in the social class variable therefore indicates an increase in average status.
4. The education variable has nine categories: (0) No qualifications; (1) Lower academic, for example, poor CSEs; (2) Lower vocational, for example, HGV licence; (3) Intermediate vocational; (4) Intermediate academic, for example, O levels; (5) Advanced vocational, for example, GNVQ; (6) Advanced academic, for example, A levels; (7) Higher vocational, for example, professional qualifications; (8) Higher academic, for example, degree
5. Earnings and parental income data are reported in 2000 prices.

Table A7(b): The impact of attrition and non-response on sample characteristics – BCS women

	Father's social class (age 5)	Reading percentile (age 10)	Maths percentile (age 10)	Poor at 16	Education category (age 30)	Poor at 30
All cohort members	3.55 (1.27) [5,874]	51.63 (28.19) [6,171]	47.85 (27.69) [5,678]	0.269 (0.444) [3,606]	4.60 (2.63) [5,703]	0.119 (0.324) [4,658]
Income at 10	3.57 (1.25) [4,711]	51.91 (27.99) [5,197]	48.08 (27.50) [4,823]	0.265 (0.441) [3,080]	4.63 (2.61) [4,601]	0.119 (0.324) [3,779]
Income at 16	3.53 (1.27) [2,850]	54.02 (28.13) [3,015]	50.22 (27.52) [2,801]	0.270 (0.444) [3,606]	4.73 (2.62) [2,939]	0.118 (0.323) [2,442]
Income at 10 and 16	3.55 (1.25) [2,491]	54.06 (28.01) [2,701]	50.32 (27.31) [2,521]	0.265 (0.442) [3,080]	4.76 (2.60) [2,529]	0.120 (0.324) [2,074]
Income at 16 and education	3.51 (1.26) [2,360]	54.87 (27.73) [2,477]	51.07 (27.26) [2,314]	0.243 (0.429) [2,933]	4.73 (2.62) [2,938]	0.118 (0.323) [2,422]
Income at 16 and income at 30	3.52 (1.27) [1,967]	54.79 (27.59) [2,047]	51.03 (27.19) [1,914]	0.244 (0.430) [2,437]	4.73 (2.64) [2,441]	0.119 (0.324) [2,422]
Income at 10, income at 16 and income at 30	3.53 (1.25) [1,722]	54.93 (27.46) [1,838]	51.09 (26.99) [1,721]	0.241 (0.428) [2,087]	4.75 (2.63) [2,091]	0.120 (0.324) [2,074]

Notes:

1. Standard deviations are in parentheses.

2. Sample sizes are in square brackets.

3. The father's social class variable has six categories: (1) Professional ; (2) Intermediate; (3) Skilled non-manual ; (4) Skilled manual; (5) Semi-skilled; (6) Unskilled. A fall in the social class variable therefore indicates an increase in average status.

4. The education variable has nine categories: (0) No qualifications; (1) Lower academic, for example, poor CSEs; (2) Lower vocational, for example, O levels; (3) Intermediate vocational; (4) Intermediate academic, for example, O levels; (5) Advanced vocational, for example, GNVQ; (6) Advanced academic, for example, A levels; (7) Higher vocational, for example, professional qualifications; (8) Higher academic, for example, degree

5. Earnings and parental income data are reported in 2000 prices.

Testing robustness to attrition

Tables A6 and A7 reveal some concerns about the selection into the final sample. As discussed in the main text we have attempted to explore the implications of this for the results by re-weighting the data. This requires developing a model that predicts whether individuals will remain in the sample or not. After experimenting, the best way of doing this appears to be to use all those in the sample at age 16 (this covers 80% in the NCDS and 62% in the BCS), and predict from this sample those who are included in the persistence of poverty samples, in other words, have income information at age 16 and age 33/30 – this means that information up to age 16 can be used to model inclusion in the final sample. Of all those in at 16, 47% of men and 49% of women are in the NCDS final samples, while 58% of men and 65% of women in the BCS are included. It is unfortunate that attrition up to 16 cannot be modelled, and this clearly may have different implications in the two cohorts.

Table A8 reports the models for men that are used to predict those who remain in the final sample. A large number of variables are used here, including information on the number of questions answered by both parents and children, information on specific missing variables, and details on ability and family background. Despite the extensive number of variables used to predict the sample selections, the models actually do rather badly, with only a limited number of variables having a significant effect, and a very small amount of explanatory power in the models as a whole.

Tables A9 and A10 show the implications for the persistence of poverty models of using the weights derived from these models to give more weight to those individuals who are less likely to be included. Comparing the weighted and un-weighted estimates shows a very limited impact from this approach to dealing with attrition and non-response. This is due to the difficulty of predicting the selection process, and can be interpreted as meaning that these difficulties should not be impacting too greatly on our conclusions. The worry remains that there are important sample selections related to unobservable aspects of individuals; to have confidence in the results we must assume that these have similar impacts in both cohorts.

Table A8: Example equations to predict remaining in the sample from age 16 to adulthood – men

	NCDS	BCS
Reading quintile 1	−0.031 (1.44)	−0.030 (1.12)
Reading quintile 2	−0.019 (0.89)	−0.006 (0.25)
Reading quintile 4	−0.009 (0.42)	0.019 (0.80)
Reading quintile 5	0.005 (0.21)	−0.002 (0.09)
Math 1	−0.038 (1.61)	0.003 (0.11)
Math 2	−0.029 (1.37)	0.029 (1.14)
Math 4	−0.001 (0.04)	0.015 (0.57)
Math 5	0.020 (0.87)	0.024 (0.89)
Reading score missing	0.027 (0.08)	−0.066 (2.01)
Maths score missing	−0.027 (0.08)	0.012 (0.39)
Mother left school 16-18	0.009 (0.52)	0.017 (0.93)
Mother left school 18+	0.007 (0.21)	−0.028 (0.97)
Father left school 16-18	0.020 (1.05)	−0.002 (0.12)
Father left school 18+	0.006 (0.18)	−0.052 (1.98)
Mother's education missing	−0.001 (0.04)	0.068 (0.62)
Father's education missing	−0.032 (0.96)	−0.090 (0.84)
One child in household	0.029 (1.25)	−0.019 (0.78)
Three children in household	0.011 (0.66)	−0.008 (0.48)
Four plus children in household	−0.001 (0.07)	−0.032 (1.50)
Number of children missing	0.092 (1.13)	−0.111 (1.30)
Lone mother age 16	0.017 (0.64)	0.066 (2.16)
Lone mother status missing	0.006 (0.02)	0.024 (0.83)
Father professional	0.024 (0.73)	0.069 (1.90)
Father intermediate	−0.034 (1.64)	−0.040 (1.80)
Father skilled non-manual	0.027 (1.14)	0.040 (1.47)
Father semi-skilled	0.017 (0.96)	−0.060 (2.50)
Father unskilled	−0.028 (1.02)	−0.058 (1.53)
Socmiss	−0.044 (2.37)	−0.016 (0.49)
Nonwhite	−0.042 (1.16)	−0.101 (2.52)
NWmiss	−0.029 (1.86)	0.059 (0.54)
1 move by 11/10	−0.007 (0.43)	0.005 (0.29)
2 moves by 11/10	−0.005 (0.24)	−0.018 (0.82)
3 moves by 11/10	−0.025 (1.04)	−0.035 (1.23)
4 moves by 11/10	−0.022 (0.94)	0.002 (0.07)
Moving information missing	−0.001 (0.02)	−0.033 (0.90)
Smokes at 16	−0.021 (1.57)	−0.064 (2.69)
Smoking information missing	0.063 (1.03)	−0.086 (3.68)
Parent answers age 11/10 questions	0.158 (2.02)	−0.012 (0.16)
Parent answers 1st age 16 questionnaire		−0.169 (4.41)
Parent 2nd age 16 questionnaire		−0.088 (3.11)
Parent 3rd age 16 questionnaire		−0.079 (4.61)
Child answers self-report at 16	−0.123 (1.39)	0.028 (0.72)
Proportion of questions child answers	0.242 (2.68)	−0.029 (0.72)
Yorks	−0.014 (0.40)	−0.045 (1.36)
North West	−0.040 (1.26)	−0.017 (0.52)
East Mids	0.030 (0.81)	−0.015 (0.42)
West Mids	−0.017 (0.51)	−0.055 (1.60)
East Anglia	−0.037 (0.79)	0.048 (1.18)
London	−0.060 (1.82)	−0.077 (2.06)
South East	−0.044 (1.47)	−0.023 (0.76)
South West	−0.059 (1.64)	−0.029 (0.85)
Wales	−0.036 (0.95)	0.023 (0.63)
Scotland	−0.014 (0.42)	0.009 (0.26)
Region miss	−0.229 (8.42)	
R-squared	0.044	0.032
Sample	7,494	5,790

Table A9: Weighted estimates of persistence from 16 to 30/33

Measures used		1958 cohort	1970 cohort
Men			
FES poverty lines at both points in time	Unweighted	2.068 (5.18)	3.943 (8.40)
	Weighted	2.110 (5.11)	3.905 (8.20)
FES proportions in poverty at both points in time	Unweighted	2.376 (5.29)	3.382 (7.83)
	Weighted	2.437 (5.22)	3.343 (7.60)
FES proportion at age 16, poverty line at age 30	Unweighted	2.086 (4.60)	3.761 (7.56)
	Weighted	2.130 (4.55)	3.786 (7.45)
Women			
FES poverty lines at both points in time	Unweighted	1.999 (5.90)	3.559 (9.77)
	Weighted	2.073 (6.00)	3.640 (9.87)
FES proportions in poverty at both points in time	Unweighted	2.123 (5.16)	3.091 (8.81)
	Weighted	2.226 (5.29)	3.138 (8.85)
FES proportion at age 16, poverty line at age 30	Unweighted	2.045 (5.07)	3.527 (8.88)
	Weighted	2.142 (5.20)	3.529 (8.82)

Note: t-statistics are in parentheses.

Table A10: Weighted estimates of persistence from 16 and 30/33 to 42

Explanatory variable	Unweighted	Weighted
Men		
Poor at 16	2.001 (4.88)	2.113 (4.95)
Poor at 16	1.662 (2.58)	1.660 (2.31)
Poor at 33	8.800 (11.14)	9.001 (10.41)
Women		
Poor at 16	2.125 (5.98)	2.141 (5.72)
Poor at 16	1.796 (3.55)	1.858 (3.61)
Poor at 42	7.966 (13.56)	8.133 (13.07)

Comparing poverty rates in the FES and cohort studies

Poverty at 16

When poverty lines drawn from the FES are applied to the cohort studies, 22% of the NCDS cohort is defined as living in poverty at age 16, compared with 26% in the BCS[2]. This can be compared with 14% of children aged between 10 and 16 in the FES in 1974 (when the NCDS information is observed) and 16% in 1986 (the relevant year for the BCS). This implies that parents may be reporting lower amounts of income in the cohort studies than they do in the FES, which is not surprising given that the questions are more detailed and precise in the FES than in the cohort studies. In recognition of this possibility, the comparable poverty rate in the FES is used to generate an alternative definition of poverty. When using this approach, the poorest 14% of the NCDS at age 16 is defined as poor and the bottom 16% of the BCS is defined as poor. Having two definitions of poverty helps to reassure us that the patterns observed in our results are not simply the consequence of data problems or the specific definitions of poverty chosen.

Table A11 summarises this information on poverty at age 16. It shows that regardless of the poverty measure used there is a small but notable increase in child poverty from one cohort to the next. Rows 1 and 2 define poverty according to the rules described above, and show the proportion in poverty increasing by two to four percentage points (information on the general rise in child poverty from 1968 to 1996 can be found in Gregg et al, 1999b). The final row in the table provides an alternative measure: the percentage of cohort members where parents respond that they are experiencing financial difficulties (as used in Gregg and Machin, 1999). By this metric, childhood poverty has increased from 10% to 15% between the cohorts.

Table A11: Childhood poverty measures

	NCDS age 16	BCS age 16
Poor (poverty line)	22%	26%
Poor (proportion of comparable FES population in poverty)	14%	16%
Parents report financial difficulties	10%	15%

Note: The poverty line is defined as 60% of the population median of equivalised family income.

---

[2] Poverty lines are equivalised income of £20.80 in 1974 and £83.09 in 1986.

Poverty in adulthood

Table A12 provides information on the proportion of adult cohort members in poverty in the surveys we use. Again two definitions are used, one based on the poverty line obtained from the FES[3] and the other based on the proportion poor of a similar group in the FES. The first thing to note is that the discrepancy between the two definitions is much smaller than for the age 16 data. This is likely to be because the method of obtaining income information for the adult cohort members is much more similar to the questions used in the FES, in that individuals are asked about the different components of income. The second feature to note is the discrepancy between the genders. At all ages and in both cohorts, women are between three and seven percentage points more likely to experience poverty than men. This is due both to their lower earnings, and the fact that they are more likely to be lone parents.

Table A12: Adult poverty measures

	NCDS age 33	NCDS age 42	BCS age 30
Men			
Poor (poverty line)	12%	12%	9%
Poor (proportion of comparable FES population in poverty)	11%	12%	13%
Women			
Poor (poverty line)	19%	15%	12%
Poor (proportion of comparable FES population in poverty)	16%	15%	17%

Note: Poverty line is defined as 60% of the population median of equivalised income.

[3] Poverty lines are equivalised income of £131.12 in 1991 and £192.35 in 2000.